Investing in Dividends

FOR DUMMIES

A Wiley Brand

Investing in Dividends

FOR DUMMIES®

A Wiley Brand

by Lawrence Carrel

Investing in Dividends For Dummies®

Published by: **John Wiley & Sons, Inc.,** 111 River Street, Hoboken, NJ 07030-5774, www.wiley.com

Copyright © 2016 by John Wiley & Sons, Inc., Hoboken, New Jersey

Published simultaneously in Canada

Library of Congress Control Number: 2015951277

ISBN 978-1-119-12195-4 (pbk); ISBN 978-1-119-12197-8 (ebk); ISBN 978-1-119-12198-5 (ebk)

Manufactured in the United States of America

10 9 8 7 6 5 4 3 2 1

Contents at a Glance

Table of Contents

Introduction

*T*he purpose of the stock market is to enable companies to raise the capital they need to start or grow their businesses. Instead of borrowing money from a bank and paying interest on it, a company can sell shares of itself to investors. Over the years, the stock market has gone from being a respectable venue for investors to purchase partial ownership in companies to something more akin to a casino. Seduced by reports of individuals earning millions nearly overnight by investing in high-growth stocks, speculative investors poured money into many companies that offered nothing more than a promise of sales and profits, further inflating share prices. When the needle point of reality finally popped the bubble, the poor unfortunates who failed to cash out their chips early enough were blown away like dust.

Fortunately, the deflated bubble (along with some dividend-friendly tax legislation) brought many investors down to earth and back to the basics — investing in companies with a proven track record of earning profits and paying dividends. As they return to the fold, investors are beginning to realize what their parents, grandparents, and great-grandparents already knew — dividend investing offers a host of benefits that provide a safer and often more profitable way to invest in the stock market.

Dividend investing is nothing new. In fact, since 1602, when the Dutch East India Company became the first corporation to issue stock, dividends have been the primary way for investors to receive profits from their investments without dissolving the company or selling the investment. However, following a dividend-investment strategy is new to many modern investors who've been focused solely on growth investing. If you count yourself among this crowd or are just starting out and plan on investing in dividend stocks, you've come to the right place. *Investing in Dividends For Dummies* contains all you need to know to develop your strategy, find and evaluate potentially good dividend stocks, manage your portfolio, and avoid the most common and critical mistakes.

About This Book

I'd love to be able to hand you a list of stocks and send you off with instructions to buy each one, but investing doesn't work that way. Every investor is different. You have a unique personality, specific goals, and a tolerance for risk that's different from your neighbors next door or across the street. Every company is different, too, operating in a specific industry, offering unique products and services, and being managed to varying levels of success. As an investor, your goal is to pair yourself up with investment opportunities that are a suitable match. That's what this book is all about.

In *Investing in Dividends For Dummies*, I present the idea of dividend investing and lead you through a process of self-examination to determine the type of investor you are, identify your goals, and develop an overall strategy that can move you most efficiently (and safely) from point A to point B. I show you how to find promising candidates and how to then evaluate them by using time-tested criteria so that you choose the best stocks to meet your needs. I mention some historically well-performing stocks you may want to check out, show you various ways to buy and sell shares, and offer guidance on managing your portfolio after you've purchased some shares.

The best part about this reference book is that *you* decide where to start and what to read. I've written every chapter to stand on its own, so you can start at the beginning of the book or pick any chapter from the table of contents and dig in.

As you read, keep one important point in mind: Past performance of a stock is no guarantee of future returns. I know, I know — you've heard that one before. But it's worth repeating. What it boils down to is this: If I mention a company in this book that I think is a potentially good dividend stock, don't assume I'm telling you to buy it. You may want to look into it, but I'm not necessarily recommending it. After all, by the time you read this book, that stallion of a stock may be a bust. Whatever you invest your money in or spend your money on is entirely your choice. I provide some guidance in picking stocks that may be likely to outperform other stocks, but I provide no specific recommendations. Take all the credit for your good investment decisions, but take all the blame for bad ones, too.

Foolish Assumptions

While writing this book, I made a few foolish assumptions, mainly about you and how much you know about investing:

- ✔ You have a general understanding of investing and your investment options, including CDs (certificates of deposit), money market funds, stocks, bonds, mutual funds, real estate, and so on.
- ✔ You grasp the basics of stock market investing.
- ✔ You realize that investing always carries some risk, that some risks are greater than others, and that *not* investing can also be risky.
- ✔ You have some money (capital) to invest. It doesn't need to be stuffed in your pocket or sitting in a bank account. It can be money you already have invested, perhaps sitting in an IRA or 401(k).
- ✔ You want a safer way to invest your hard-earned dollars, so you're interested in introducing or adding more dividend stocks to your portfolio.

Icons Used in This Book

Throughout this book, you can spot icons in the margins that call your attention to different types of information. Here are the icons I use and a brief description of each:

Everything in this book is important, but some of it's more important. When you see this icon, read the text next to it not once but two or three times to brand it on your brain cells.

Tips provide insider insight from behind the scenes. When you're looking for a better, faster, safer, and/or cheaper way to do something, check out these tips.

This icon appears when you need to be extra vigilant or seek professional help before moving forward.

Investing has its fair share of highly specialized language and concepts that typically fly above the heads of mere mortals. Whenever I explain something highly technical, I flag it with this icon so that you know what's coming.

Beyond the Book

In addition to all the material you can find in the book you're reading right now, this product also comes with some access-anywhere goodies on the web. Check out the Cheat Sheet at www.dummies.com/cheatsheet/investingindividends for helpful insights and details about whether you should hire a financial advisor and considerations for building a nest egg. You can also find interesting companion articles at www.dummies.com/extras/investingindividends.

Where to Go From Here

Investing in Dividend For Dummies is designed to appeal to a universal audience of intermediate and experienced investors at all stages of developing and managing their investment portfolios.

For the new dividend stock investor, I recommend you read the book from cover to cover starting with Chapter 1. More experienced divided stock investors who already know themselves and their goals and have an effective strategy in place to reach those goals may want to skip to Chapter 7, where I show you how to track down income-generating, dividend paying stocks, or Chapter 8, where I show you how to evaluate them.

Regardless of your experience, however, feel free to skip around and read whatever catches your interest. Each and every tidbit of knowledge and insight you acquire can only serve to make you a more astute investor.

Part I
Getting Started with Dividends

Visit www.dummies.com for more great Dummies content online.

In this part . . .

- ✔ Get the basics on the risks and rewards of dividend stocks as you prepare to become a savvy investor.

- ✔ Find out what to look for as you invest and how to adapt as the holdings in your portfolio develop.

- ✔ Discover stock market indexes and the interplay between dividends and market.

- ✔ Understand what to look for when you're looking for sound companies to invest in.

- ✔ Delve into some of the reasons that the popularity of dividend investing tends to rise and fall.

Chapter 1

Wrapping Your Brain Around Dividend Investing

* *

In This Chapter

▶ Understanding dividend stocks and their benefits and risks

▶ Preparing to become a savvy dividend stock investor

▶ Knowing what to look for as you shop for dividend stocks

▶ Monitoring and adjusting the holdings in your portfolio

* *

*F*or many investors, dividend stocks offer the best of two worlds: a healthy balance of risk and return. Investors receive the benefits of both share price appreciation and the ability to realize profits through *dividends* (cash payments) without having to sell shares. (Later in this chapter, I list more of the many benefits of dividend stocks, and in Chapter 3, I explain them in greater detail.)

In this chapter, I pack the essentials of dividend investing into a nutshell, starting with the bare basics, such as defining what a dividend is, and taking you to the very end — managing your portfolio after you populate it with promising dividend stocks. Along the way, I reference other chapters in this book where you can find additional information and guidance on each topic.

Coming to Terms with Dividend Stocks

Dividend stocks are stocks that pay dividends — payments in cash (usually) or shares (sometimes) to stockholders. Through dividend payments, a company distributes a portion of its profits to its shareholders, typically every quarter or every month, and pumps the remaining profits back into the company to fuel its growth.

The percentage of total profits a company pays out in dividends to shareholders is called the *payout ratio*. For more about payout ratios and how to use the number in evaluating dividend stocks, check out Chapter 9.

Why companies pay dividends

Successful companies are profitable companies. They earn money, and they can use that money in several ways:

- ✔ **Reinvest it:** Companies usually invest a good chunk of their profits, if not all of them, into growing the business.

- ✔ **Pay down debt:** If, in addition to selling shares, companies borrowed money to raise capital, they may use profits to pay down the debt, thereby reducing the expense of their interest payments.

- ✔ **Buy back shares:** Companies may use profits to buy back shares that they feel are undervalued, or for other reasons. In some cases, they initiate buybacks to artificially inflate the share price and improve investor confidence in the company.

- ✔ **Pay dividends:** Paying dividends is a form of *profit sharing* — spreading the wealth among the company's owners, the shareholders.

A company's dividend policy generally reflects the board of directors' and shareholders' preferences in how to use profits. Two schools of thought govern their decision:

✔ **Pro growth:** This school believes a company is better off reinvesting its profits or using profits to pay down debt or buy back shares. This strategy makes the company more valuable, and the share price rises accordingly. Shareholders benefit when they sell their shares for more than they paid for them.

✔ **Pro profit-sharing:** This philosophy stems from the belief that shareholders own the company and should share in its profits.

Other factors can also influence dividend policies. For example, the Jobs and Growth Tax Relief Reconciliation Act of 2003 (JGTRRA), which lowered the maximum tax rate on dividends from 39.6 percent to 15 percent, led companies making up the S&P 500 Index to boost their dividend payments. For more about how tax legislation can affect dividends, check out Chapters 3 and 11.

The advantages of dividend investing

Receiving dividends is like collecting interest on money in a bank account. It's very nice but not exciting. Betting on the rise and fall of share prices is much more exhilarating, especially when your share prices soar. Placing excitement to the side, however, dividend stocks offer several advantages over non-dividend stocks:

✔ **Passive income:** Dividends provide a steady flow of passive income, which you can choose to spend or reinvest. This attribute makes dividend stocks particularly attractive to retirees looking for supplemental income.

✔ **More stable companies:** Companies that pay dividends tend to be more mature and stable than companies that don't. Startups rarely pay dividends because they plow back all the profits to fuel their growth. Only when the company has attained a sustainable level of success does its board of directors vote to pay dividends. In addition, the need to pay dividends tends to make the management more accountable to shareholders and less prone to taking foolish risks.

✔ **Reduced risk:** Because dividends give investors two ways to realize a return on their investment, they tend to have a lower risk-to-reward ratio, which you can see in less volatility in the share price. A stock with lower volatility sees smaller share price declines when the market falls. Low volatility may also temper share price appreciation on the way up.

✔ **Two ways to profit:** With dividend stocks, your return on investment (ROI) increases when share prices rise and when the company pays dividends. With non-dividend stocks, the only way you can earn a positive return is through share price appreciation — buying low and selling high.

✔ **Continued ownership while collecting profits:** One of the most frustrating aspects of owning shares in a company that doesn't pay dividends is that all profits are locked in your stock. The only way to access those profits is to sell shares. With dividend stocks, you retain ownership of the company while collecting a share of its profits.

✔ **Cash to buy more shares:** When you buy X number of shares of a company that doesn't pay dividends, you get X number of shares. If you want more shares, you have to reach into your purse or pocket to pay for them. With dividend stocks, you can purchase additional shares by reinvesting all or some of your dividends. You don't have to reach into your pocket a second or third time. In most cases, you can even enroll in special programs that automatically reinvest your dividends.

✔ **Hedge against inflation:** Even a modest inflation rate can take a chunk out of earnings. Earn a 10-percent return, subtract 3 percent for inflation, and you're down to 7 percent. Dividends may offset that loss. As companies charge more for their products (contributing to inflation), they also tend to earn more and pay higher dividends as a result.

✔ **Positive returns in bear markets:** In a bear market, when share prices are flat or dropping, companies that pay dividends typically continue paying dividends. These dividend payments can help offset any loss from a drop in share price and may even result in a positive return.

✔ **Potential boost from the baby boomers:** As more baby boomers reach retirement age and seek sources of supplemental income, they're likely to increase demand for dividend stocks, driving up the price. Nobody can predict with any certainty that this will happen, but it's something to remain aware of in the coming decades.

The risks

There's no such thing as safe investing, only safer investing. You can lose money in any of the following ways:

✔ **Share prices can drop.** This situation is possible regardless of whether the company pays dividends. Worst-case scenario is that the company goes belly up before you have the chance to sell your shares.

✔ **Companies can trim or slash dividend payments at any time.** Companies aren't legally required to pay dividends or increase payments. Unlike bonds, where failure to pay interest can put a company into default, a company can cut or eliminate a dividend any time. If you're counting on a stock to pay dividends, you may view a dividend cut or elimination as losing money.

Most companies try their best to avoid these moves because cutting the dividend may cause shareholders to sell, lowering the share price.

✔ **Inflation can nibble away at your savings.** Not investing your money or investing in something that doesn't keep pace with inflation causes your investment capital to lose purchase power. With inflation at work, every dollar you scrimped and saved is worth less (but not worthless).

Potential risk is proportional to potential return. Locking your money up in an FDIC-insured bank that pays an interest rate higher than the rate of inflation is safe (at least the first $100,000 that the FDIC insures), but it's not going to make you rich. On the other hand, taking a gamble on a high-growth company can earn you handsome returns in a short period of time, but it's also a high-risk venture.

Prepping Yourself for the Journey Ahead

People often invest more time and effort planning for a weekend vacation than they do preparing to become an investor. They catch a commercial for one of those online brokerages that makes investing look so easy, transfer some of their savings to the brokerage or roll over their IRA (individual retirement account), and try to ride the waves of rising investment sentiment to the land of riches.

A more effective approach is to carefully prepare for the journey before taking the first step. The following sections serve as a checklist to make sure you have everything in place before you purchase your first dividend stock.

Gauging your risk tolerance

Every investor has a different comfort zone. The thrill-seekers crave risk. They want big returns and are willing to take big risks to get them. Riding the rollercoaster of the stock market doesn't bother them, as long as they have some hope they'll end up on top. On the other end of the spectrum are conservative investors willing to trade high returns for stability. Prior to investing in anything, you can benefit by determining whether you're more of a thrill-seeker, a conservative investor, or someone in between.

In Chapter 7, I offer several methods for gauging risk tolerance, but regardless of which method you choose, you should account for the following factors:

- ✔ **Age:** Younger investors can generally take bigger risks because they have less money to lose and more time to recover from lousy investment decisions.

- ✔ **Wealth:** "Never bet money you can't afford to lose" is good advice for both gamblers and investors. If you're relying on the money you're investing to pay your bills, send Johnny to college, or retire soon, you're probably better off playing it safe.

✔ **Personality:** Some people are naturally more risk-tolerant than others. If you tend to get worried sick over money, a low-risk approach is probably more suitable.

✔ **Goals:** If your goal is to reap big rewards quickly, you may conclude that the risk is worth it. If your goal is to build wealth over a long period of time with less chance of losing your initial investment, a slow, steady approach is probably best.

Only you can determine the right balance of risk and reward for you and your goals. You can obtain valuable guidance from a financial advisor, but how you choose to invest your money is entirely up to you (at least it should be).

Choosing the right approach

Tossing a bunch of ticker symbols into a hat and drawing out the names of the companies you want to invest in is no way to pick a dividend stock. Better approaches are available, as presented in the following sections.

Value

The value approach is like shopping at garage sales. Investors hope to spot undervalued stocks — stocks with share prices that appear to be significantly lower than what the company is really worth. When hunting for values in dividend stocks, investors look for the following:

✔ **Strong earnings growth:** Companies that earn bigger profits with each passing year demonstrate they're growing and thriving. A shrinking profit usually means trouble — bad management decisions, increasing competition, or other factors chipping away at the company's success.

✔ **High yields:** *Yield* is the ratio of annual dividends per share to the share price. If shares are selling for $50 each and dividends are $2.50 per share (annually), the yield is $2.50/$50.00 = .05 or 5 percent. Stocks with higher yields deliver higher dividends per dollar invested. For example, a dividend stock with a yield of 5 percent generates a nickel for every dollar invested, whereas a yield of 25 percent generates a quarter per dollar.

✔ **Low price-to-earnings ratio (P/E):** *P/E* tells you how many dollars you're paying to receive a share of the company's profits. If a company earns an annual profit of $3.25 for each share of its common stock and the shares sell for $50, the P/E is $50/$3.25 = 15.39. In other words, you're paying $15.39 for every dollar of profit the company earns. The P/E ratio provides a barometer by which to compare a company's relative value to other companies and the market in general. (Head to Chapter 2 for more on common stock.)

A good P/E ratio is one that's lower than the P/E ratios of comparable companies. As a general rule, investors look for P/E ratios that are lower than the average for a particular index, such as the S&P 500 or the Dow Jones Industrial Average (DJIA). See Chapter 2 for more about these stock market indexes; Chapter 9 explores P/E ratios in greater depth.

✔ **Solid history of raising dividend payments:** Like strong earnings growth, covered earlier in this list, a solid history of raising dividend payments demonstrates that the company is thriving. Every year it has more wealth to share with investors.

✔ **Solid balance sheet:** A *balance sheet* is a net worth statement for a company, listing the cost of everything it owns and subtracting the cost of everything it owes. Ultimately, a healthy balance sheet shows that the company has enough assets to cover its liabilities and then some. The remainder is called *shareholder equity.* For more about balance sheets, flip to Chapter 9.

✔ **Sufficient free cash flow:** Ideally, a company's cash flow statement shows that the company brings in enough actual cash each quarter to more than cover its expenses as well as the dividend distributions.

Growth

The growth approach to investing in the stock market focuses on a company's prospects for generating future earnings. These companies are expected to see their revenues and profits grow at a pace faster than the rest of the market. As such, this approach tends to be more speculative than the value approach. Growth investors may pay more for shares than their past results or actual performance justifies.

With the growth approach, value isn't the key variable. Although P/E ratios remain important, growth investors are willing to pay a higher price for shares than value investors. Because growth investors look to share price appreciation for returns, they're more likely to focus their attention on companies that don't pay dividends. They want younger companies that reinvest their profits to accelerate the growth rates of future earnings and revenues. If the company continues to exhibit strong growth, the share price should move significantly higher. Growth investors are well advised to consider the following:

- **Revenue growth:** Although earnings (profits) can grow through cost cutting, revenue growth demonstrates the company's sales are increasing.

- **Projected growth:** Projected growth consists of analysts' estimates of the percentage the company's revenues will grow in a year. These projections always carry some uncertainty, but investors should still take them into consideration.

- **Profit margins:** If the company reports a profit, growth investors want to see profits and revenues growing on a steady basis. Profits not keeping pace with growing revenues may be a sign that the company's profit margin is suffering.

- **Realistic share price projection:** Generally speaking, growth investors consider investing in companies only if they have a realistic expectation that the share price will double no later than five years down the road. The key word here is "realistic." Investors must base projections on data rather than gut feelings.

Income

The goal of income investing is to obtain a steady and relatively secure income stream. When purchasing equities, focusing on income means buying stocks that pay dividends. Because most growth companies don't pay dividends, most income investors are basically value investors that not only want to buy at a good price but also look for a high yield and a history of rising dividend payments. The income investor looks for companies well equipped to not only continue paying dividends but to also increase the cash amount of those payments.

Working with a seasoned pro

This book should give you the tools to manage your portfolio by yourself. However, if you do decide to hire an investment advisor, I urge you to consult a qualified professional with a track record of *successfully* investing in the stock market for several years.

Experienced investment advisors can offer you a wealth of advice and information on most areas of financial planning, including taxes, insurance, and strategies that have been successful for them. They can also function as a sounding board when you need feedback on a stock you're thinking of buying or selling and help steer you clear of potential pitfalls.

 If you don't want to pay a fee for an investment advisor's advice, consider joining an investment club where you can pool your capital to create a more diversified portfolio than you can on your own. You can also bounce ideas off fellow club members before making any investment decisions. The extra eyes and ears may have information about a company that convinces you to move forward or step back from a particular transaction. They also provide a good source of investment ideas you may not have previously considered.

Selecting First-Rate Dividend Stocks

A good dividend stock isn't just one that pays a high dividend. The strength and consistency of the dividend are very important, along with share price and the company's prospects for a rosy future. Before you can evaluate and select dividend stocks, however, you need to identify a few promising candidates.

Distinguishing dividend stocks from the rest of the pack

Wherever you find stocks, you can find dividend stocks:

> ✔ Google Finance at `www.google.com/finance`
>
> ✔ Yahoo! Finance at `http://finance.yahoo.com`
>
> ✔ Various personal finance magazines and websites
>
> ✔ *The Wall Street Journal*
>
> ✔ *Financial Times*
>
> ✔ This book!

Many stock listings include both a dividend column and a dividend yield column. If the company hasn't paid a dividend, you see something like 0.00 or a hyphen (-). Some listings show only the previous and current share price and the single-day and year-to-date gain or loss. In that case, you need to dig deeper to find out whether the company pays dividends and the amount of the most recent payment. With most online stock listings, you simply click the ticker symbol for more information about the company.

Exploring sectors where dividend stocks hang out

Companies in certain industries, such as utilities and telecoms, are more likely to pay dividends than companies in other industries, including technology and biotech. The biggest reason for this tendency is that some industries have larger, more established companies, compared with industries that have a higher concentration of smaller, growth-oriented companies.

As you begin investing in dividend stocks, you may want to focus your efforts on the following sectors:

> ✔ **Utilities:** Electricity, water, and natural gas (suppliers, not producers)
>
> ✔ **Energy:** Oil, natural gas (producers, not suppliers), and Master Limited Partnerships (MLPs)
>
> ✔ **Telecoms:** Carriers (U.S. and international) and wireless
>
> ✔ **Consumer staples:** Food/beverages, prescription drugs, household products, tobacco, and alcohol

Prior to the mortgage meltdown that started in 2007, real estate and financials would have been at the top of the list. Both sectors were traditionally good for dividend stocks. The fiscal crisis caused many to cut or eliminate their dividends. Since then, some financial and real estate companies have resumed paying dividends, but many have not.

Crunching the numbers

Eeny, meeny, miny, moe is no way to pick dividend stocks. Savvy investors carefully inspect the company reports — balance sheet, income statement, and cash flow statement — and crunch the numbers to evaluate the company's performance, at least on paper. As you prepare to evaluate a company, research the following figures or calculate them yourself by using numbers from the company's quarterly report. (Chapter 9 shows you how.)

- ✔ **Current dividend per share (DPS):** The quarterly cash payment each investor receives for each share of company stock he or she owns.

- ✔ **Indicated dividend:** The projected annual dividend for the next year, assuming the company pays the same dividend per share for each quarter of the next year.

- ✔ **Dividend yield:** A ratio that compares the amount the company pays out in dividends per share to its share price. You use yields to gauge a dividend's rate of return. Yields move inversely to share price — that is, yields go up when share prices go down (and vice versa).

- ✔ **Earnings per share (EPS):** The portion of a company's profit allocated to each share of stock. If XYZ Company sold 2 million shares of stock and earned a profit of $1 million, it earned 50 cents per share, or $1 million/2 million shares = $0.50. A company that earns $1 per share is twice as profitable as the one that earned 50 cents a share.

- ✔ **Price-to-earnings ratio (P/E):** The ratio of the share price to the annual earnings per share, which tells you how many dollars you need to invest to receive a dollar of the company's profits.

- ✔ **Payout ratio:** The percentage of a company's net profit it pays to shareholders in the form of dividends. The payout ratio indicates whether the company is sharing more of its profits with investors or reinvesting it in the company.

✔ **Net margin:** The ratio of net profits to net revenues, indicating the percentage of each dollar of sales that translates into a profit. High net margins typically indicate that a company has little competition and large demand for its products. This situation allows the company to charge a high price for its products or services.

✔ **Return on equity (ROE):** The ratio of a company's annual net profit to shareholder equity, ROE provides some indication of how effective a company is turning investor dollars into profits.

✔ **Quick ratio:** An indication of a company's liquidity or ability to meet its short-term financial obligations. The higher the ratio, the more likely it can afford to pay dividends moving forward.

✔ **Debt covering ratio:** An indication of whether a company has sufficient operating income to cover its current liabilities, including payments on debt.

✔ **Cash flow:** The difference in how much actual cash comes into the company during the quarter versus how much it pays out. A company can make a lot of sales in a quarter, but if clients don't pay their bills, no cash comes into the firm.

Don't evaluate a company based on one value. The numbers work collectively to paint a portrait of the company's current financial status. For additional guidance on interpreting these values, see Chapter 9.

Performing additional research and analysis

Numbers paint a fairly detailed portrait of a company's current financial status and can even be used to some degree to forecast the company's future performance. Numbers, however, provide no context. They may indicate potential problems or opportunities, but they don't reveal what's causing those problems or making those opportunities available. They provide little indication of the company's management philosophy or expertise; or outside factors, such as the state of the economy, what's going on in the sector, and what analysts and investors think of the company's prospects.

To find out everything you need to know to make a wise decision, you have to do some research. Here are some suggestions to find out more information about the companies you're thinking of investing in:

- ✔ **Read the quarterly earnings reports of the companies you're thinking of investing in.** Every public company is legally obligated to file these reports with the U.S. Securities and Exchange Commission (SEC) — the federal regulator of Wall Street.

- ✔ **Research companies on the Internet.** You can usually find plenty of information on the company's website, in online financial publications, and on sites such as Yahoo! Finance and Google Finance. Use your favorite search engine to search for the company by name.

- ✔ **Check out the competition online, too.** Which company is leading the pack; what's it doing that the others aren't?

- ✔ **Read reports written by stock analysts at investment banks.** These analysts spend a lot of time each quarter investigating whether companies are performing up to their own expectations.

- ✔ **Subscribe to and read financial publications online or off.** Sorry, but not everything is available for free on the Internet — you usually have to pay for the best information, whether you get it online or in print.

- ✔ **Check out what other investors have to say.** Many investors maintain blogs that provide useful insights and can give you some sense of investor sentiment.

Blogs may provide insight, but *never* base an investment decision on a blog or comment from an investor. These people may have an agenda that conflicts with yours. Some people talk up stocks on Internet chat boards and blogs to raise the share price on the stocks they own so that they can cash out.

Building and Managing Your Portfolio

When you evaluate individual companies, you're involved in what can best be described as identifying the best pieces for an investment puzzle. When you actually buy shares to assemble a portfolio, you shift to a more "big picture" perspective. Although you must micromanage the portfolio by keeping an eye on each investment, you also need to evaluate how each investment fits into your master plan and ultimate investment goals.

Settling on a stock-picking strategy

Every investor has a unique investment strategy for spinning straw into gold. Usually the best approach is a combination of several strategies to achieve the right balance of risk and return while efficiently reaching the investor's goal.

Any general in the military can tell you that strategies don't always unfold as planned on the battlefield, but not having a strategy in place is pure folly. Develop the best strategy possible, but keep in mind as you move forward, that you may need to adjust it.

The following are some semi-famous strategies that investors have developed for picking dividend stocks:

- ✔ **The Dogs of the Dow:** In 1991, Michael O'Higgins proposed an investment strategy called *The Dogs of the Dow* based on the fact that a dividend stock's yield rises whenever its share price drops. Proponents of this theory believe that the components of the Dow Jones Industrial Average with the highest dividend yields have the greatest potential for capital appreciation in the coming year.

- ✔ **The Geraldine Weiss Approach:** Geraldine Weiss, editor of *Investment Quality Trends* (www.iqtrends.com), is a leading expert on dividend investing who promotes buying high-yield blue-chip stocks. The overall strategy is to buy high and sell low — that is, buy when dividend yields are at the historic highs and sell when the dividend yields hit historic lows. Sticking with blue-chips helps avoid financially troubled companies.

✔ **Relative Dividend Yield:** Developed by money manager Anthony Spare, this approach rates stocks by comparing a company's dividend yield to that of the average yield of the S&P 500. In his book *Relative Dividend Yield: Common Stock Investing for Income and Appreciation,* 2nd Edition (Wiley), Spare recommends giving careful consideration to stocks with a dividend yield that's more than double the average on the S&P 500.

✔ **Dividend Achievers:** Dividend Achievers identifies companies that have an outstanding track record for increasing dividend payments every year. To make it on the U.S. Broad Dividend Achievers Index, U.S. companies must have at least ten consecutive years of increasing regular dividends, be listed on the NYSE or NASDAQ, and have a minimum average daily cash volume of $500,000.

Limiting your exposure to risk

In the world of investing, risk is an ever-present reality, but you can implement several strategies to limit your exposure:

✔ **Education and research:** Knowledge is power, and by reading this book, you're already engaged in the pursuit of the requisite insight and know-how.

✔ **Dollar cost averaging:** *Dollar cost averaging* is investing a fixed amount of money at regular intervals (such as monthly) toward the purchase of a particular investment. With dollar cost averaging, sometimes you pay more for the investment and sometimes less. This strategy reduces your chance of paying a premium for a large number of shares and then losing a huge amount of money when the price drops.

✔ **Diversification:** Don't put all of your golden goose eggs in one basket by investing heavily in any one company, sector, or type of investment. By diversifying your portfolio with stocks, bonds, and cash, you not only spread the wealth but also lower your risk profile.

> ✔ **Strategic timing:** No, I'm not recommending that you try to time the market. What I do recommend is that you match your investment strategy to your time frame. Be aware of how many years you have before you need this money. The less time you have, the more conservative your investments should be. As you get older, consider allocating a higher percentage of your portfolio to safer investments, such as bonds, to protect your capital.

Buying and selling shares

After dealing with all the preliminaries, including settling on an investment strategy and carefully researching individual stocks, you're almost ready to start trading. Almost, because you need to address one more preliminary — how you're going to go about buying and selling shares. You basically have three options:

> ✔ **Direct:** You may be able to purchase shares directly from the company. For more about direct purchase programs, see Chapter 6.
>
> ✔ **Broker:** Brokers buy and sell shares on commission. In other words, they execute trades on your behalf. A full-service broker charges more but may offer some valuable insight and advice. A discount broker merely processes your order. If you're a do-it-yourselfer, this route is the way to go.
>
> ✔ **Investment advisor:** A registered investment advisor is a step above a broker. An advisor can help you build and manage a portfolio to meet your financial goals, recommend stocks and other investments to consider, and meet with you regularly to make adjustments.

Reviewing your portfolio regularly

In the best of all possible worlds, you can build your portfolio and let it set sail without a care in the world. In the real world, you must continue to invest at least some time and effort reviewing your portfolio and making adjustments. Monitoring dividend stocks consists of reevaluating them regularly, using the same criteria you used to select them in the first place: dividend, yield, price-to-earnings ratio, payout ratio, and so on. When you notice the performance of one of the stocks in your portfolio slipping or have reason to believe it will start slipping, you may need to replace it with a better prospect. In addition, you probably want to make adjustments to your portfolio as your goals change. At the very least, you should check your portfolio twice a year to make sure your asset allocations match your strategy.

Don't fall asleep at the wheel. Companies, even large, well-established companies, can run aground. Remain vigilant and jump ship before that happens.

Staying on top of possible tax code changes

Tax legislation can make investing in dividend stocks more or less attractive. For many years, dividends were taxed as ordinary income — at a rate as high as 39.6 percent. In other words, for every dollar in dividends, investors had to fork over about 40 cents to Uncle Sam. In 1981, when the rate on long-term capital gains was reduced to a maximum of 20 percent, many investors shifted from dividend to growth stocks to give themselves a tax cut.

The Jobs and Growth Tax Relief Reconciliation Act of 2003 (JGTRRA) changed all that. It dropped the tax rate on long-term capital gains and dividends to a maximum of 15 percent, leveling the playing field.

Tax legislation can be a game changer, and Congress can change the rules at any time. Remain vigilant to protect yourself from unfavorable tax legislation and to take advantage of favorable legislation. Remember, the less you pay in taxes, the more you get to keep and even reinvest.

Checking Out Various Investment Vehicles

Investment vehicle is a fancy term used to describe an investment product other than basic stocks or bonds. Sometimes it refers to a product, such as a fund, which holds many different stocks or bonds. Other times, it refers to a way to purchase stocks or bonds other than a straightforward purchase. Some examples are

- ✓ **Dividend reinvestment plans (DRIPs):** Many companies that pay dividends allow investors to enroll in DRIP programs, which automatically reinvest dividends to purchase additional shares. This strategy is usually a great way to compound returns.

- ✓ **Direct stock purchase plans (DSPs):** DSPs allow you to purchase shares directly from the company rather than through a broker, which can save you some money on commissions and fees. They're also called *direct purchase plans,* or DPPs.

- ✓ **Dividend-focused mutual funds:** The main benefit of a dividend-focused mutual fund is the same as that for any mutual fund — it provides an easy way to diversify your holdings. In exchange, you relinquish your control over picking individual stocks to the mutual fund manager.

- ✓ **Exchange-traded funds (ETFs):** An ETF is basically an index mutual fund that trades like a stock. Quite a few ETFs focus on dividend investing.

- ✓ **Foreign dividends:** Some foreign companies pay dividends, too, and with foreign dividend investment vehicles, you don't even have to worry about trading in your yens, euros, and shekels for dollars.

Chapter 2

Brushing Up on Dividend Details

. . . .

In This Chapter

▶ Taking a look at stock market indexes

▶ Getting up to speed on dividend stock basics

▶ Understanding how dividends influence the stock market

▶ Raising your awareness of key dates affecting dividend payments

. . . .

*A*s an investor, you may think you need to know only two facts about dividend stocks: that some companies pay dividends and some don't. However, knowing a few additional details about these stocks can make you a much savvier and more confident investor.

In this chapter, I cover the nuts and bolts of how dividends work and bring you quickly up to speed on the two main indexes that reflect the stock market's overall health. I explain a few key concepts, including yield, and explore factors that contribute to making one dividend stock a better choice than another. I also explain some key dates that affect when companies pay dividends, which may influence your decision of when to buy and sell shares.

The Major Stock Market Indexes

People measure the health of the stock market by using various indexes. An *index* is sort of like a thermometer for a market. When business is good, the index tends to rise. When business is bad, it falls. Thousands of indexes measure every industrial sector in the United States and business performance in every country in the world. To take the temperature of the energy sector or the financial sector, you can find an index specifically for those industries. If you want an index of just dividend stocks, you can find that too.

Two major indexes measure the broad market: the Dow Jones Industrial Average (DJIA) and the Standard & Poor's 500 Index. These indexes are known as the stock market's *benchmarks*. They not only measure the health of the stock market but also provide a historical basis from which you can derive data, gain valuable perspective on what's going on in the markets, and draw conclusions. When the media say the stock market is up or down, they mean the Dow and the S&P 500 are up or down. When they say the market is mixed, they mean these two indexes are going in opposite directions. The indexes are important to you because most of the stocks on them pay dividends.

I reference these indexes throughout this book, so you should know what each index represents and how they differ. If I refer to one index more than another in a particular discussion, I do so only because the index I'm referring to provides more or better data to illustrate the point under discussion. In the section "The Role Dividends Play in the Market" later in this chapter, I use these indexes to reveal the impact that dividends have had on the stock market over the past hundred years or so.

In addition to these two long-time barometers, the NASDAQ Composite Index has become a benchmark for the NASDAQ Stock Market. Most pertinent, I don't deal with the NASDAQ because the majority of its components don't pay dividends.

Dow Jones Industrial Average

Invented in 1896 to track just 12 companies, the Dow Jones Industrial Average is the best-known stock market index in the United States. It goes by a few nicknames, such as the Dow Industrials and the DJIA, but most people know it simply as the Dow. Today, the Dow consists of just 30 companies in the major industries in the United States.

Critics complain that the sample of 30 companies is too small to serve as an accurate measure of the stock market's performance and that its price weighting doesn't take into account the sizes of the companies in the index. However, the Dow has been measuring the stock market for almost 120 years, which gives it a lot of credibility.

Price weighting values companies based on their share price, not total market value. As its name says, the Dow is an average. So a company with a share price of $50 makes up five times more of the index than a company with a share price of just $10, even if the lower priced stock produces twice the profits or has more shares trading in the market.

Standard & Poor's 500

Better known, as the S&P 500 or just the S&P, the Standard & Poor's 500 Index holds 500 of the largest companies in the United States, but not necessarily the top 500. Created in 1957, the S&P is considered a more representative index because it holds about one-tenth of all the publicly traded companies. More importantly, this tenth of the market's companies collectively represents about 75 percent of the stock market's total dollar value.

The index weights the companies based on their value in the market — a value measured by the company's *market capitalization*:

Market Capitalization = Share Price × Number of Outstanding Common Shares

For example, in early 2009, ExxonMobil was the largest company in the index, with a market capitalization of $338 billion. It held an index weighting of 4.86 percent. AT&T, the second-largest company, wasn't quite half the size of Exxon, with a market capitalization of just $148 billion, so its weighting of 2.14 percent was less than half of Exxon's weighting. Giving larger companies more influence over the index makes the S&P 500 a more accurate measuring tool for the broad market.

When I call the shares *outstanding,* I'm not referring to the strength of the company or any other positive characteristic. *Outstanding stock* tells you the number of shares the company has sold to investors and can now trade on the market.

The Difference Between Common and Preferred Stock

To raise capital, companies can issue two types of stocks: common and preferred. Each type or class of stock offers different rights, benefits, and restrictions.

Common stock

When people talk about stocks, they typically mean *common stock,* the most popular and widely held type of equity. When I refer to *stock,* I mean common stock.

Compared to preferred stock (see the following section), common stock offers the following advantages and disadvantage:

- **Advantage:** Holders of common stock share in the company's profits through increasing dividends and a rising share price. Common shareholders elect the board of directors and vote on broad corporate issues such as mergers.

- **Disadvantage:** Shareholders receive the last claim on earnings and the company's assets. In other words, if the company goes bankrupt, you receive your payment after all the creditors and preferred stock holders get paid. In almost every bankruptcy, common shareholders get nothing.

Preferred stock

As its name implies, preferred stock holds advantages over common stock. However, its disadvantages actually outweigh its advantages in most cases. Following are some of the advantages preferred stock offers shareholders:

- **Fixed dividends:** Dividend payments remain more stable, which can be an advantage in times when the company is having trouble making a dividend payment but a disadvantage when dividends rise. Often the yields are higher than common dividends and the corporation's bond interest rates.

- ✔ **Payment priority:** Holders of preferred stock are first in line to receive dividends. In other words, they receive their dividends before holders of common shares receive theirs. With *cumulative preferred stock,* if the company has unpaid and overdue debts to the preferred share-holders, all the unpaid preferred dividends must be distributed before the common shareholders receive a penny. If the firm is in serious trouble (little cash, no assets to sell for cash, and no ability to borrow to pay the dividend), the dividend may have to *accrue* (accumulate).

- ✔ **Greater claim to any of the company's assets:** In the event of a bankruptcy and ensuing liquidation, holders of preferred shares receive any money left over before hold-ers of common shares receive any money. In liquidations, common shares often become worthless.

Preferred shares also carry some considerable disadvantages:

- ✔ **Fixed dividends:** Although a fixed dividend payment can be an advantage when the company fails to earn a profit, it also means the dividend payment doesn't rise when the company earns bigger profits. Fixed payments also make the shares interest-rate sensitive. If interest rates rise, the share price may fall in order to boost the yield. I explain how yield works later in this chapter.

- ✔ **Less share price appreciation:** Because the dividend is fixed, the price of preferred shares is based on the yield they offer. As a result, preferred shares actually trade more like a bond than a stock.

- ✔ **No voting rights:** Holders of preferred shares have less say than common stock holders in how the company is managed and who sits on the board of directors.

In short, holders of common stock assume more risk but stand to gain more when the company is profitable.

You can usually tell the difference between a company's common and preferred stock by glancing at the ticker symbol. The ticker symbol for preferred stock usually has a *P* at the end of it, but unlike common stock, ticker symbols can vary among systems; for example, Yahoo! Finance lists pre-ferred stock with the company's ticker symbol followed by a hyphen, the letter *P,* and then the series letter (for example, J.P. Morgan preferred is JPM-PE), whereas Google Finance includes only the series letter (without the *P,* JPM-E).

Company Fundamentals

You've probably heard a few success stories about investors tossing darts to choose the companies they invest in or kids assembling a portfolio that significantly outperforms the S&P 500. Stories like these may be entertaining, but they often send a dangerous message that picking good stocks is a random, hit-or-miss activity. On the contrary, consistently successful investors do their homework and crunch the numbers. They carefully inspect each company's *fundamentals,* including the following:

- ✔ **Revenue:** Total amount of money the company received from sales

- ✔ **Expenses:** Total amount of money the company spent to generate income

- ✔ **Net Profit:** Revenue minus expenses; also called *earnings*

- ✔ **Assets:** Cash value of everything the company owns

- ✔ **Liabilities:** Cash value of everything the company owes

- ✔ **Debt:** Total amount of money the company owes to lenders; a kind of liability

- ✔ **Cash flow:** Positive if the company brings in more actual cash than it paid out; negative if the company spent more cash than it brought in

In Chapter 9, I show you how to perform a fundamental analysis of a company based on the company's quarterly reports, including its balance sheet, income statement, and cash flow statement.

Fundamental analysis focuses on a company's financial metrics; *technical analysis* examines share price in an attempt to forecast future share prices based on the charting of historical trends and market conditions. I encourage you to give more credence to fundamentals and less to technicals.

Paying Tribute to Yields

One of the easiest and fastest ways to determine the relative value of a particular dividend stock is to look at its *yield* — the ratio of dividends per share to the share price. For example, if shares are selling for $25 each and dividends are $2.50 per share (annually), the yield is $2.50 ÷ $25 = .10 or 10 percent.

The yield is the magic number. Yield tells you the percentage rate of return you can expect from the dividend, making it very useful in comparing the returns you can expect from different investment options. However, yield isn't the sole factor in determining the comparative value of dividend stocks. When you sell your shares, whether the share price rose or fell, and by how much, also contributes to the total return on your investment.

The Role Dividends Play in the Market

In the stock market, share prices command all the attention. You hear about how much the share price of General Electric or Ford or Google rose or fell. You hear analysts pitching their best guesses on whether a particular stock's value will rise or fall. What you rarely hear about are dividends, and that's unfortunate given the impact that dividends have had and continue to have on the market.

Dividends' contributions to returns

Total return measures a stock's total performance from both dividends and share price appreciation. If a stock starts the year at $50 and pays a $4 annual dividend, the dividend yield is 8 percent: $4 ÷ $50 = 8 percent. If the stock gained $6 to end the year at $56 (up from $50), it saw *capital appreciation* (increase in value based on its market price) of 12 percent:

$6 ÷ $50 = 12 percent

Add the dividend yield and capital appreciation together, and you get the total return of 20 percent. (Total return of an index over many years often includes the reinvestment of the dividends on an annual basis.) I explain how reinvesting dividends annually affects total return in Chapter 3.

From January 1926 to December 2008, the S&P 500 Index (and its predecessors) delivered an annualized total return of 9.69 percent per year. The shocking aspect of that is that over those 83 years, *price appreciation* (rising share prices) accounted for only 5.5 percentage points of that 9.69 percent. Dividends actually accounted for the remaining 4.19. In other words, dividend income comprised 43.27 percent of the S&P's returns:

4.19 percent ÷ 9.69 percent = 43.27 percent

The numbers from the Dow paint a similar picture. From January 1, 1930, (about two months after the crash of 1929) to December 31, 2008, the cumulative return on the Dow was 5,914.64 percent or 7.96 percent on an annualized basis. Price appreciation accounted for just 4.62 of that 7.96 percent points, and dividends accounted for the other 3.34. Looking at it another way, dividend income comprised about 41.96 percent of the Dow's total returns:

3.34 percent ÷ 7.96 percent = 41.96 percent

An *annual rate of return* is the return for a 12-month period, such as January 1 to December 31. An *annualized rate of return* is the rate of return for a period longer or shorter than one year. The number is either multiplied or divided to determine an equivalent return for a one-year period.

Dividends made up 43.27 percent of the S&P's total return and 41.96 percent of the Dow's total return. These numbers are pretty consistent and clearly indicate that if you forgo dividends, you give up more than 40 percent of the potential profits you can derive from the stock market.

Investment returns in the form of dividends take on even greater importance in a bear market. In bear markets, stocks can go for years without posting any significant capital gains, but companies often continue to pay dividends. Dividends may provide the only returns you receive when share prices drop or flatline.

To gain a clearer perspective, take a look at the Dow Jones Industrial Average over the period from January 1, 1999, to December 31, 2008. During this period, the stock market experienced some serious ups and downs — the rally of

the technology bubble that peaked in early 2000, the ensuing crash that bottomed out in 2002, the rally of the housing
bubble that lifted stocks to an all-time high in 2007, and then a
plunge of more than 50 percent in 2008 through early 2009.

We can explore what would have happened if you had
invested $100 in the Dow stocks on the last day of 1998.
By the end of 2008, based on share price appreciation alone,
that $100 would be worth $95.59, representing a return
of –4.41 percent. Including dividends, however, the total
return would be $117.95 — a nearly 18-percent profit on your
investment and a 22.36-percentage point jump over price
appreciation alone. And that doesn't even include reinvesting
the dividends!

The positive effects of dividends on stock prices

In the midst of investor irrationality, dividends tend to calm
the raging stock market seas by injecting some sanity into
the marketplace in a couple of ways. First, they make managers more accountable to shareholders. Shares of growth
companies can be particularly vulnerable to price fluctuations. Obsessed with growth and lacking the accountability to
shareholders that dividends provide, managers often spend
profits to acquire businesses that don't fit strategically with
their main business. This disregard can send stock prices
soaring when investors believe the acquisitions will increase
profits, but disappointments can have the opposite effect,
sending share prices to the cellar. Plummeting share prices
sometimes give back more than 90 percent of their previous
gains. Having to pay dividends encourages managers to be
more sensible in their acquisitions and provides them with
less cash to squander on poor decisions.

Second, dividend payments provide steadier returns to investors. Even when stock prices are in a freefall, shareholders
can usually count on receiving their dividend payments. This
dependability not only calms the nerves of potentially anxious
shareholders but also gives them more capital to reinvest in
the company or in other companies, which can help further in
stabilizing the stock market.

Important Dates in the Life of a Dividend

Dividends aren't paid like clockwork. Unlike other forms of income-generating investments, companies have no legal obligation to pay dividends. This fact means the company's board of directors must actively declare, every single quarter, whether it will pay a dividend.

Because dividend stocks, like all other stocks, can be traded on the open market, companies need some way to determine who (the buyer or the seller) gets the next dividend payment when shares are exchanged. You may assume that the person who owned the shares the longest during the quarter would get the dividend payment. After all, if you own the shares for 10 of the 12 weeks that comprise the quarter, you should have more right to the dividend payment than the investor who owned the shares for just the other 2 weeks, right? Well, not exactly.

When you buy and sell dividend stocks, dates determine who gets the dividend and who doesn't. To determine the rightful recipient of dividend payments, companies keep track of several dates in the life of a dividend share, including the date of declaration, trade date, settlement date, date of record, ex-dividend date, and the actual payment date. Because each dividend is a unique event, the company must specify the important dates for this payment. In the following sections, I explain in more detail how these dates are used to determine the rightful recipient of the dividend payment.

Date of declaration

The *date of declaration* is the date on which the company's board of directors announces its next quarterly dividend payment. The declaration typically begins with something like this:

> Chicago, IL — January 29, 2011 Carrel Industries, a provider of consumer products, today announced that its Board of Directors has declared a quarterly cash dividend on its common stock of 44.5 cents per share. The dividend

is payable on February 27, 2011, to stockholders of record on February 13, 2011. Carrel Industries initiated quarterly cash dividend payments in the third quarter of fiscal year 2005 and has increased the dividend by 5 percent from the dividend level one year ago.

In this example, the date of declaration is January 29, 2011. The declaration also contains two more key dates: the *payment date* (February 27, 2011, in the example) and the *date of record* (February 13, 2011, in the example). I explain these two dates a little later in this chapter.

Trade date

Stock trading is a lot like buying or selling a house. You buy the house one day but you don't actually become the official owner until after the closing. With all stocks, the day you buy your shares is the *trade date*, but you don't actually take ownership of the shares until several days later on the settlement date, described in the following section.

Settlement date

The *settlement date* (also called the *closing date*) is the date on which the transaction becomes finalized — the buyer pays for the securities and becomes the official shareholder of record while the seller relinquishes her ownership status and collects the money. For equities, the settlement date is the trade date plus three business days (known as T + 3). The seller has three business days after the trade date to deliver the shares to the buyer.

Rarely do investors receive actual stock certificates to prove ownership, as they did in the good old days. Instead, companies keep electronic records of transactions to facilitate the process of trading shares. The person holding possession of the shares according to these company records is called the *shareholder of record.*

Date of record

The *date of record* is the cut-off date for dividend payment eligibility. In other words, to receive the next scheduled divided payment, your name needs to be on the company's books as the shareholder of record on or before the date of record. If you buy and close on shares before the date of record, you receive the dividends. If you buy before the date of record but settle after it, the seller receives the dividends because she's listed as the official owner on the date of record.

Ex-dividend date

Ex-dividend means "without dividend," so the ex-dividend date determines the payment of dividends on the purchase and sale of shares.

- **Purchase:** Buy shares before the ex-dividend date, and you qualify for the declared dividend. Buy shares on or after this date, and you're ineligible for the most recently declared dividend.

- **Sale:** Sell shares on or after the ex-dividend date, and you collect the declared dividend. Sell shares before this date, and you miss out on the payment.

The ex-dividend date is arguably the most important date to the dividend investor, but the press release rarely mentions it.

So where does this all-important ex-dividend date come from? After a company chooses the date of record, the stock exchanges or the National Association of Securities Dealers, Inc., sets the *ex-dividend date* two days prior to the date of record. This system creates a three-day period before the date of record during which anyone buying shares is ineligible to receive the declared dividend payment. Why three days? Because a trade on or after the ex-dividend date settles after the date of record.

Because the dividend returns value to the shareholder, ex-dividend also means that the dividend is value removed from the stock's price, meaning the dividend stock typically trades lower on the ex-dividend date. So, if a company's shares close at $10 the day before the ex-dividend, and the dividend is 25 cents a share, on the morning of ex-dividend the stock opens up at $9.75.

Don't base your decision to buy or sell solely on whether you'll be eligible for the declared dividends. Consider both the share price and the yield to determine what's in your best interest.

Payment date

The *payment date* (also referred to as the *distribution date*) is many shareholders' favorite day. On this date, the company distributes dividends to shareholders. Most companies pay dividends after the end of each three-month fiscal quarter. When a company's fiscal year aligns with the calendar year, the fiscal quarters end on the following dates:

- ✔ **First quarter:** March 31
- ✔ **Second quarter:** June 30
- ✔ **Third quarter:** September 30
- ✔ **Fourth quarter:** December 31

A company's fiscal year may not align with the calendar year. For example, the calendar year runs from January 1 to December 31, but a company's fiscal year may run from August 1 to July 31 or October 1 to September 30.

Chapter 3

Grasping the Dividend Advantage

*Y*ou can put your money into all sorts of investments, such as stocks, bonds, mutual funds, real estate, and commodities. Each investment carries its own potential risks and rewards, and each can play a unique role in your investment strategy.

Because this book focuses on dividend-paying stocks, I'm not about to discuss your overall investment strategy or the pros and cons of each type of investment vehicle. Instead, this chapter focuses specifically on the advantages (and a few possible drawbacks) of dividend-paying stocks — stocks that not only change in value but also pay a portion of the company's profits to the shareholder, assuming, of course, the company is profitable. I also reveal some of the reasons dividend stocks fell out of favor and have staged a comeback.

The Pros and Cons of Investing in Dividend Stocks

Prior to investing in anything, savvy investors examine the risk/reward profile to determine whether they want to take a chance and roll the dice. Although dividend stocks are generally less risky than non-dividend stocks (for reasons I explain in the following section), they do carry some risk and may not hold sufficient promise of rewards for some investors. To make a well-informed decision of whether dividend stocks are right for you, evaluate the pros and cons, as described in the following sections.

This is your money, so don't let anyone, including me, tell you how to invest it. As the investor, you need to determine whether the pros outweigh the cons or vice versa. As I explain in the later section "The Rise and Fall of Dividend Stocks' Popularity," dividend stocks can become a more- or less-attractive option as conditions change.

Exploring the pros

As you may have guessed, I have a strong preference for stocks that pay dividends over those that don't, and for good reason. In the following sections, I describe the many benefits of investing in dividend stocks.

Gaining two ways to win

With dividend stocks, you have two ways to win: when the share value rises and when the company cuts you a dividend check, paying you a portion of its profits. If the share price rises by 4 percent, and the company pays a 3-percent dividend, you pocket a 7-percent profit, minus taxes, of course. (Or you can reinvest your dividends to buy more shares. See "Compounding returns via reinvesting" later in this section.)

In addition to providing two ways to win, the share-price-plus-dividend advantage allows you to hedge your bet. If share prices fall by 4 percent and the company pays a 3-percent dividend, you lose only 1 percent of your investment. Of course, companies can always choose to slash dividends, so you're not completely safe, but you're often safer than if you're relying solely on rising share prices to score a profit.

Securing a steady stream of income

Investors often talk about the beauty of passive income. Instead of having to work to earn a buck, you put your money to work for you. Dividend stocks enable this dream to come true. You buy shares, and as long as the company is profitable and paying dividends, you have a steady source of income without having to lift a finger.

With most other investments, you don't realize a profit until you sell. Before you tell a broker to sell, any profit is a *paper profit* — you can see it on a statement, but you can't spend it or stick it in your piggy bank. If your investment drops in value, that profit can go "poof!" Just ask anyone who held shares of Enron before news of its scandal broke.

Dividend stocks are different. Companies pay out the dividends in cold, hard cash. These aren't paper profits that can disappear in a bear market. Dividends are money in your pocket, and after they're paid they can't be taken from you.

Companies typically pay dividends on a regular basis — usually every fiscal quarter (three months).

Achieving profits and ownership

If your stocks don't pay dividends, the only way you can wring cash out of your investment is by selling your shares. Unfortunately, selling shares means relinquishing your ownership in the company — something you may not want to do if you think the company will grow and the share prices will rise. With dividends, you receive a return on your investment while holding onto the shares for potential capital appreciation.

Compounding returns via reinvesting

Compounding is one of the most powerful forces in the world of investing. It's like the old riddle: How much wheat do you end up with if you place one grain of wheat on a checkerboard square and then double the amount each time you move to the next of the 64 squares? Answer: Enough grain to bury India 50 feet deep! That's a little exaggerated in terms of investing, but compounding returns follows the same principle.

Suppose two investors, Party Pete and Frugal Frank, each own 100 shares of company ABC Inc. at $20 a share, a $2,000 investment. Each receives a dividend of $2 per share — a 10-percent yield that gives them $200 at the end of the first year (100 shares times $2). Party Pete uses the $200 to take his wife out for a fun night of dinner and theater. Frugal Frank uses his $200 to buy 10 new shares of ABC Inc. Now Frank owns 110 shares.

Note: Most stocks pay quarterly dividends, but to make this example easy to understand, I'm assuming one dividend payment of $2 a year rather than four quarterly payments of 50 cents.

The next year the dividend remains at $2. Pete receives another $200 and again spends the money to have fun with his wife. Frank now receives $220 (110 shares times $2). He reinvests his dividends again. Now he can buy 11 new shares, giving him a total of 121 shares.

After the third year the dividend is still $2. Party Pete receives another $200 and uses it to go away for a weekend trip. Meanwhile, Frugal Frank now receives a payment of $242. He uses this money to buy 12 new shares, giving himself a total of 133 shares.

After the third dividend gets paid, the stock's price jumps to $25. Both Pete and Frank decide to sell all their shares. Who earned more? Frugal Frank, of course! Here's how the numbers break down:

On the initial investment of 100 shares bought at $20 each, both Pete and Frank made $500.

Sale Price	$25/share × 100 shares	= $2,500
Subtract		
Initial Investment	$20/share × 100 shares	= $2,000
Price Appreciation	$5/share × 100 shares	= $500

To figure out each investor's total return you need to add in the dividends.

Because Pete didn't reinvest any of his $200 dividend but took it all in cash, he received a total of $600 in dividends. Together with his capital appreciation, he earned $1,100:

Price Appreciation ($500) + Dividends ($600) = Total Return $1,100

Because Frank reinvested his dividends, each year he had more shares on which dividends were paid. For the three years, his dividends totaled $662. This means Frank earned $62, or 10 percent, more than Pete in dividends alone.

Dividends $200 + $220 + $242 = $662

Over the three years, Frank reinvested $660 of these dividends to buy 33 more shares at $20 each. When he sold these additional shares for $25, he received $825, for an additional profit of $165. This gave him a total return of $1,327

Price Appreciation ($500)

+ Dividends ($662)

+ Appreciation from shares bought with reinvested dividends ($165)

Party Pete's sale of his original 100 shares, for a $5 profit per share, gave him $500 in capital appreciation, for a 25-percent return from price alone: $500 ÷ $2,000 = .25. Add in the $600 in dividends ($200 a year in dividends for three years) and Party Pete's total return (dividends plus price appreciation) comes to $1,100, for a total rate of return of 55 percent: $1,100 ÷ $2,000 = .55.

Meanwhile, doing nothing but reinvesting his dividends, Frugal Frank earned $1,327, or 20.6 percent more profit than Party Pete. This gave Frugal Frank a total rate of return of 66.4 percent in just three years: $1,327 ÷ $2,000 = 0.664.

Hedging against inflation: Another way to WIN

In August 1974, then-president Gerald R. Ford encouraged his fellow Americans to Whip Inflation Now (WIN). Inflation was at about 11 percent back then, and just about everybody in the country was wearing a WIN button. One of the best ways to keep inflation from taking a bite out of your investment earnings is to invest in dividend-paying stocks. The big advantage dividends hold over other income generating investments is they have the potential to keep pace with inflation. As prices rise, profits also tend to rise, and companies can afford to raise their dividend payments.

Inflation takes a bite out of earnings. With inflation at a modest 3 percent, a 7-percent annual return on an investment (not bad) nets only a measly 4-percent annual gain.

When you account for inflation, stock appreciation from 1926 to 2008 is pretty dismal. Over that period, the S&P 500 earned an annualized total return of 9.69 percent per year. Of that percentage rise, dividends accounted for about 4.19 percent, and price appreciation accounted for 5.5 percent. Subtract 3 percent for inflation, and stock appreciation alone produced an annualized average return of only 2.5 percent.

The Dow is even worse. Of its annualized total return of 7.96 percent, dividends accounted for 3.34 percent, and share appreciation contributed 4.62 percent. Subtract 3 percent for inflation, and investors who counted solely on stock appreciation for earnings realized an annual return of only 1.62 percent.

Banking on the buy-and-hold advantage

Dividend investors tend to be more committed than non-dividend investors. They're in the market for the long haul and want to own shares in companies that deliver returns in good times and bad. As a result, dividend shares tend to outperform non-dividend shares when the market heads south. Several factors contribute to this trend:

- ✔ When stock prices are falling, investors are under pressure to sell to either secure their gains or limit their losses. As more and more investors sell their shares, prices drop even more, often triggering a vicious cycle that drives share prices even lower.

- ✔ Investors typically sell their dividend stocks last. They hold onto those stocks longer because dividend stocks continue to give them a return on their investment.

- ✔ The fact that many dividend stock investors don't sell tempers any decline in the share price.

> ✔ Investors burned by the large losses from their high vola-
> tility stocks look for safer, more stable investments. They
> may move their money into dividend stocks to protect
> their gains (with a safer investment) or as a way to cap-
> ture some returns in a bad environment for price appre-
> ciation. Greater investor demand can drive up the share
> price of dividend stocks even as the rest of the market
> stagnates. This situation creates a *profit circle:* Greater
> demand pushes a stock price higher, which creates
> greater demand, which pushes the price even higher.

Stocks that offer only capital appreciation through rising
stock prices have little chance of providing a positive return
when stock prices are falling. Thus, many investors sell these
stocks sooner than dividend stocks.

Riding the possible baby boomer retirement surge

In the preceding sections, I discuss the classic advantages of
investing in dividend stocks. Another factor may contribute to
the success and stability of dividend stocks: the graying of the
baby boomers, those 77.3 million people born in the United
States between 1946 and 1964. Beginning in the 1980s, this
demographic has had a tremendous influence on the stock
market and will continue to into the foreseeable future.

This huge sea of workers has begun retiring. By 2030, the
Congressional Budget Office expects the number of people
in the United States ages 65 and older to approximately
double, according to the office's November 2003 report "Baby
Boomers' Retirement Prospects: An Overview."

In order to maintain their preretirement lifestyle in retirement, baby boomers will need to rely on their investments
to supplement their income. This necessity will likely cause
many to change their investment strategies from one primarily focused on growth to an income-based approach.
Translation: Boomers face an increasing need to score
supplemental income, and the smart ones who have money
to invest are likely to consider dividend stocks as a prime
source of that supplemental income. Traditionally, retirees
tend to reposition their assets into more conservative portfolios that focus on income generation over capital appreciation through growth. Nobody has any reason to believe that
this trend will change when the boomers retire. Assuming
this scenario happens, both stock prices and dividends
should rise accordingly.

Investigating the cons

Whenever you sign on the dotted line with a broker, mutual fund manager, or other intermediary, he usually presents you with a long disclaimer that basically boils down to a single statement: "Past results are no guarantee of future performance." In other words, yesterday's winner can be tomorrow's loser. Investing always carries risk, and dividend stocks are no exception. A few dangers to be aware of:

- ✔ In general, dividend-paying companies see less price appreciation than growth stocks.

- ✔ Share prices can drop whether the stock pays dividends or not.

- ✔ Companies can slash or eliminate their dividend payments at any time for any reason. As a shareholder, you're at the end of the line when checks are cut.

- ✔ Tax rates on dividends can rise, making dividend stocks a less attractive option — for the company to pay and for you to receive.

Not investing also carries risk. If you stuff your money in a mattress or bury it in a coffee can in the backyard, someone can steal it or mice, bugs, or inflation can eat away at it.

Investing in Solid Companies

When you see that a company is doling out healthy dividends to shareholders, you know it has positive cash flow — more cash is flowing in than flowing out. The company can cover its bills, compensate its employees, pay its taxes, and still have some money left over to distribute to investors. Perhaps even more important, dividends typically are a sign that the company is fundamentally sound, which means it should exhibit the following qualities:

- ✔ Maturity
- ✔ Effective management
- ✔ Stability
- ✔ Earnings growth

In the following sections, I describe these qualities of fundamentally sound companies in greater detail and point out some of the early warning signs that crop up when a company or an entire sector starts experiencing problems.

Just because a company looks good on paper and is paying dividends doesn't guarantee it's healthy. Underlying issues may be chipping away at the company's foundation before signs of trouble appear. A company with negative cash flow from operations can hide its troubles by borrowing money, selling off assets, or issuing new stock. These moves are short-term fixes that the company can't sustain or hide for long. You can reduce your risk through careful research and diversification, but you can never eliminate it entirely.

Maturity: Boring, but stable

As I mention in Chapter 1, dividend stocks evoke a mental image of Grandma's portfolio and, like Grandma, most of the companies that pay out dividends are what you'd probably call *mature*. They're settled in. They may have slowed down a bit in terms of growth, but they're rock-steady.

Companies proceed through various stages of life, just like people:

- ✔ **Infancy:** Startup companies typically have great prospects but require more money and attention to get up and running. During a company's infancy, it's probably spending more money than it's earning, but its low share price and potential for big profits are attractive to growth investors. Without an influx of sufficient cash to fuel their growth, companies at this stage risk becoming like malnourished children, and their growth can be stunted.

- ✔ **Childhood:** Assuming a company survives its infancy, it typically develops quickly. At the childhood stage, revenues often grow in leaps and bounds as well, but the risk factor for investing in the company remains high.

- ✔ **Teenage:** During this stage, companies can be as different as any two teenagers. Some are fairly mature. They earn enough to cover their expenses and perhaps even a little surplus. They make good choices. They're fairly independent. Other companies are accidents waiting to happen: irresponsible, misdirected, accident-prone, ready to take risks without carefully evaluating the situation, and constantly needing more and more capital just to stay afloat. Companies at this stage generally still have plenty of growth potential, but poorly managed companies have more potential for failure.

✔ **Adulthood:** Mature companies are like adults. They've done most of their growing already. Mature companies still raise profits, but typically at a slower rate. Although they may not see big year-over-year advances in share price and profits, their long experience has taught them effective, efficient ways to earn money consistently. You can always find exceptions, but a mature company is one that generally takes fewer outrageous risks to score big.

Strive to become a mature investor, too. The novice is often eager to scoop up shares of growth companies in their infancy or early childhood in the hopes the share price doubles or triples in a short period of time. In their irrational exuberance, these novice investors may fail to account for the risk factor — the more you stand to gain, the more you stand to lose (generally speaking). I'm not saying that investing in companies in their infancy is necessarily bad, but it's typically riskier than investing in an established company with a proven track record.

Good management

Dividends typically signify good corporate management. To pay out a dividend, a company must have cash on hand. Management can't fake it. It can (and sometimes does) fake paper profits by padding its sales and profits on reports, but it can't fake paying cash dividends to shareholders. Paying dividends over a long period of time makes a positive statement about the company's financial health. When you see a company paying dividends, you can expect the following:

✔ **Management confidence:** Paying a dividend provides a clear signal about management's confidence in the company's ability to continue to post profits.

✔ **Fiscal discipline:** The decision to pay a dividend isn't entered into lightly. As soon as a company starts paying a dividend, shareholders come to expect it. Cutting or eliminating a dividend reflects very poorly on the managers and the company in the eyes of investors.

✔ **Corporate governance:** Dividends provide a form of corporate governance for shareholders. Corporate managers, by the nature of their positions, know more about a company's operations than do outside shareholders. Contemporary corporate scandals show that some managers make decisions to benefit themselves at the expense of the company and its true owners, the shareholders. Because companies can't fake dividends, payments provide a good benchmark for shareholders.

✔ **Earnings transparency:** In light of earnings-manipulation scandals, paying dividends validates the company's accounting process and increases the credibility of the earnings reported currently and in the past. Again, you can fake sales and earnings figures, but you can't fake cold, hard cash.

In addition, paying dividends subjects companies to certain checks and balances. Companies that pay out dividends need to be more judicious with how they spend shareholder money. They have less cash on hand to undertake corporate investments or acquisitions of other companies. Should a dividend-paying corporation decide to make a large investment or acquisition, it has to go to the capital markets, for either debt or equity, to fund the project. When companies seek outside money, investors and other interested outside parties scrutinize the plans and can often derail anything they deem foolish or overly risky. In other words, dividends make management more accountable to investors.

Public and private organizations sell either debt or equity to raise capital to fund their operations. The stock and bond markets, collectively known as the _capital markets,_ are where capital is sold and traded.

Stability

Dividend companies typically provide for the necessities of life: food, water, electricity, gas, a place to live, and the

all-important personal hygiene. As a result, the classic industries for dividends include the following:

- ✔ Utilities
- ✔ Real estate
- ✔ Energy
- ✔ Finance
- ✔ Telecommunications
- ✔ Consumer staples, such as food and clothing

Because people always purchase these products and services,
even when times are tough, the industries that provide them
are generally more stable. Less stable companies provide
what consumers can live without — computers, cellphones,
digital music players, restaurants, and anything travel related,
such as hotels and airlines.

You're probably about to jump out of your seat and scream
"Financials? Real estate? Stable? Not going out of business?
Are you crazy?" Yes, I know that during the stock market
bubble that peaked in 2007, financials broke the mold of
stable companies and went bonkers themselves. I know that
many ran their companies poorly and with little shareholder
oversight even as they paid out dividends. And yes, I know
that many financial institutions went bankrupt, losing lots of
money for investors. But please stay seated.

Every rule has exceptions. Yes, many financials broke the
rules, but the red flags were waving before the bubble burst,
and attentive investors who knew the warning signs bailed
out early. Overall, however, dividend companies are more
stable than non-dividend companies. In fact, paying dividends
is probably one factor that helped some financial companies
survive the crash, assuming they didn't have to take money
from the government.

Don't buy shares and then fall asleep at the wheel. Take nothing in the stock market for granted. It's always moving, so
remain vigilant. In this chapter and throughout this book, I
show you how to assess the health and growth potential of
companies before purchasing shares. Use these same strategies to reevaluate your holdings regularly: I recommend at
least annually, if not quarterly.

Strong earnings growth

Investors often think mature companies pay out a large portion of their profits as dividends because they can't find investments that offer good returns in their traditional businesses. Reality offers a more nuanced view. Take a look at General Electric (GE). You can't find a more mature company than GE or one that had increased dividend payments more consistently. Yet the company pumped a good portion of its earnings into growth and diversification, building and running 12 major business units in state-of-the-art technology, from jet aircraft engines to household appliances.

Early warning signs

Companies that pay dividends are generally more stable than companies that don't, but they're not always more stable, as became obvious with the downfall of the financial sector in 2008. Until that time, financial companies, in general, had a long and strong reputation for paying sizeable dividends. The sector's demise serves as a reminder that there's no such thing as a safe sector or a safe stock. Even General Electric, which owns a huge financial unit that got hurt in the subprime mortgage debacle, was forced to cut its dividend in 2008 for the first time since the Great Depression.

Many people who bet big on the financial sector were skewered, but many attentive and knowledgeable investors moved their money before tragedy struck, because they spotted the early warning signs — indications of trouble below the surface that you can't see just by looking at annual reports, share prices, or dividends. When investing, you need to remain attentive and know what to look for, including the following signs of trouble:

- Problems in the company's main business
- Declining sales
- Falling profits
- Rising debt
- Negative cash flow
- Dividend cuts

✔ Declining health of the industry

✔ Negative news stories about the company or industry

✔ Investigations by regulators or the police

✔ Declining economic conditions

✔ Chief executive contracting a serious illness

The Rise and Fall of Dividend Stocks' Popularity

Throughout this chapter, I present dividend stocks as the next best thing to winning the lottery, but this scenario isn't always the case. For various reasons, dividend stocks become more or less attractive. For example, earlier in this chapter I discuss the likelihood that baby boomers, looking for a stable source of supplemental income, may significantly increase demand for dividend stocks. Other factors may also come into play to further strengthen or weaken demand.

In the following sections, I point out the key factors that may affect the popularity of dividend stocks so that you're aware of conditions that can increase or decrease the net return on your dividend investments.

Dividends fall out of favor

For most of the 20th century, dividends accounted for about half of the stock market's return — approximately 40 percent, to be precise. Yet, in the year 1999, dividends had fallen to account for only about 7 percent of the market's total returns. Why did investors turn their backs on this easy, relatively consistent money? A combination of factors over the last two decades of the 20th century led investors to treat dividends as second-class citizens:

✔ **Dividend-bashing tax laws:** A dramatic change in the tax laws sparked dividends' sudden fall from grace. In 1981, tax rates on long-term capital gains were cut to a maximum of 20 percent, and dividends continued to be taxed at an investor's tax rate for ordinary income, which ran as high as 70 percent! Before the long-term capital gains tax cut, Standard & Poor's says 94 percent of the S&P 500's component stocks paid out more than 50 percent of their earnings in dividends. By 2002, only 70 percent of companies on the S&P 500 paid dividends. On average, the dividend payout ratio was slashed nearly in half to 30 percent of profits.

✔ **Double taxation:** Dividends are taxed twice, both at the corporate and individual levels — a practice known as *double taxation.* Coupled with changes in the tax code, this double taxation took an even bigger chunk out of dividends. Even older, mature companies, the kind that historically paid dividends, changed their dividend policies. With price appreciation receiving more tax benefits than dividends, companies decided to focus on increasing shareholder value through price appreciation.

✔ **Growing popularity of growth investing:** When dividend investors realized that taxes were taking a good chunk out of their earnings, many changed strategies. Do the math and you quickly realize that paying 20 percent on long-term capital gains beats paying nearly 40 percent on dividend income. The changes in the tax code sparked a rush into investments with the potential for huge price appreciation. Most of these investment dollars moved into small, growth-oriented companies that didn't pay dividends. This capital infusion was a major factor in the bull markets of the 1980s and the 1990s.

✔ **Growth company boom:** During the bull market, the number of new companies entering the stock market soared. The U.S. economy was firing on all cylinders. With astronomical growth in the high tech industries of computer technology, telecommunications, and the Internet, the U.S. stock market's value grew by nearly 1,000 percent. With price gains like this, investors weren't interested in waiting around 20 years to see results they could achieve in less than 12 months.

✔ **Share buybacks:** Companies cut dividends and used the excess capital to buy back their shares on the open market, thus lowering the number of shares available for purchase. This reduction isn't necessarily a negative for shareholders. Share buybacks send a message to the market that management believes the stock is underpriced. Buybacks boost a stock's price by creating more demand for shares. Buybacks can also boost the earnings per share by lowering the amount of shares outstanding.

Dividend stocks stage a comeback

The popping of the stock market's technology bubble in 2000 sent stock prices into a two-year freefall. Many technology companies went out of business. With nothing to show for their investments in growth companies, investors shifted to plan B. Suddenly the concept of earning profits in the form of dividends didn't seem so old-fashioned to investors. This time, the combination of factors showed how fleeting price appreciation can be:

✔ **Dividend-friendly tax laws:** The Jobs and Growth Tax Relief Reconciliation Act of 2003 has had the most influence on the increasing popularity of dividend investing. This tax law cut taxes on both dividends and long-term capital gains to 15 percent. This change made dividend income much more attractive. In the wake of the tax cut, dividend payouts on the S&P 500 jumped by an average of 8 percent. Dividend stocks helped spur the bull market of 2003 to 2007. With no taxation penalty, dividends gained equal footing with long-term capital gains and reemerged to their rightful place in the investment universe.

✔ **Buybacks backfire:** The buybacks that typically lift share prices had some unintended consequences. Many firms used this technique to boost the price of shares that had fallen significantly in value. In essence, a company would use the buybacks to prop up falling share prices, sending Wall Street a false signal that management was confident in the company's future. When investors failed to buy into the buyback, the company was sunk — if it was cash-poor before, it was flat broke after buying back all those shares.

✔ **Earnings scandals:** The stock market crash of 2000 also exposed the dirty underbelly of the bull market. Many companies weren't growing as fast as their management proclaimed. In fact, many were losing money. Realizing the only reason their investors stayed with them was for price appreciation, corporate managers broke the law to keep share prices, and hence their salaries, rising. Executives manipulated their companies' financial statements and perpetrated fraud to show bigger and faster profit growth than actually occurred. Some of the largest companies in the country — Enron, WorldCom, and Adelphia — were destroyed by earnings scandals. Investors learned the hard way that profits, but never dividends, can be faked.

✔ **Second stock market bubble pops:** Investors who didn't see the writing on the wall in 2000 received a repeat lesson on the value of dividends with the 2008 financial crisis. With stock market indexes plunging more than 50 percent off their highs, investors saw the unrealized profits in their portfolios disappear like smoke into the air twice in one decade. Thus, the steep declines in share prices and beneficial changes in the tax laws have made investing in dividend stocks much more attractive.

Part II
Exploring the World of Dividends

In this part . . .

- ✔ Look into specific industries to consider as you build your portfolio.

- ✔ Find out what utility and energy stocks have to offer, or what telecoms and consumer good sectors can bring.

- ✔ Gauge the potential of banks and real estate investment trusts, and investigate some notable options.

- ✔ Check out some of the many ways you can invest in dividends, like dividend reinvestment plans (DRIPs), mutual funds, and exchange-traded funds (ETFs).

Chapter 4

Income-Generating Industries

In This Chapter

▶ Exploring what constitutes a utility — and what makes an attractive one

▶ Revving up your portfolio with energy stocks

▶ Taking advantage of master limited partnerships (MLPs)

▶ Checking out what telecoms have to offer

▶ Discovering what the consumer goods sector offers

*S*ome sectors (industries) are better than others at delivering a steady stream of income to shareholders. Companies in the consumer staples sector, for instance, have a better track record for paying dividends than do companies in the biotechnology industry. Likewise, utilities generally trump technology.

This chapter introduces you to the best sectors for dividend investing so that you can focus on individual sectors and diversify your portfolio. For each industry, you discover the types of companies included in that sector, why companies in the sector are more likely to pay dividends, and how to size up companies in the sector.

Don't follow recommendations, even mine, until you perform your own due diligence. Back in the 1990s, the financial and real estate sectors were attractive, but starting in 2008, that was no longer the case. Individual companies and entire sectors can run into problems, so do the research and analysis I describe in Chapter 8.

Lighting Up Your Portfolio with Utilities

Utilities are a category of companies that provide the services and power necessary to run buildings and make modern life possible. Given their propensity to pay out 60 to 80 percent of their average annual earnings as dividends, utilities are some of the highest-yielding stocks in the entire stock market. (For more about yield, see Chapter 9.) The following sections give you the lowdown on utility stocks and their benefits.

Which companies qualify

Companies in the utilities sector provide electricity, gas, heat, and water. These capital-intensive industries boast significant ownership of facilities (such as power and water-treatment plants) and infrastructure (such as power lines and pipes) that run overhead and under streets and into homes and businesses. The three main classes of utilities are

- **Electric companies** are responsible for the generation, transmission, and distribution of electrical power. Integrated utilities provide all these functions under one roof. Generation can involve a variety of sources, including gas, nuclear energy, solar power, and wind power, but the burning of coal still generates more of America's electricity than any other source. Transmission and distribution rely on power grids and power lines. Although many states have deregulated their electricity markets, when generation and transmission come from two separate companies, both fall into the utilities category.

- **Natural gas companies** provide the energy to heat homes and supply cooking gas. They're often aligned with electric companies because gas is also used to produce electricity. Most natural gas companies remain monopolies, which means that these companies almost always earn a profit and pay dividends but also that they can be subjected to heavy regulation. The following section covers the effects of monopolies and regulation on utilities in greater detail.

✓ **Water companies** are responsible for distributing fresh water throughout communities, piping it into buildings, and removing sewage. Most water companies are owned or run by the local municipalities. However, water supplies are running scarce in parts of the United States and the world. Supplies are expected to tighten, providing earnings growth potential as demand exceeds supply.

Utilities' income-generating capabilities

The classic regulated utility makes a great income-generating stock because profits are practically guaranteed. Yet, due to governmental regulations, these earnings experience little to no growth. Limited profit growth significantly lowers the potential for capital appreciation in utilities' stock prices. These companies need another way to give shareholders a return on the equity invested, so they entice investors by promising to pay high yields (through dividends) equal to or above the rate of Treasury bonds. Here are a few reasons utilities traditionally have been good income-producers:

✓ **They're monopolies with no competition.** Building power plants and infrastructure requires huge capital investments, and it is neither practical nor desirable to have numerous power grids or sewage systems overlapping each other. The huge capital requirements create a big barrier to other firms entering the business; few companies would commit so much money without some assurance they'd receive a return on their investment. (Recent experiments with deregulation to foster competition among generating plants have shown companies are unwilling to take on this kind of investment without a guaranteed customer base.)

✓ **Government-set rates ensure a reasonable profit.** Regulators need to balance the competing interests of shareholders with the needs of consumers. Although customers need rates to remain affordable, the utility must remain profitable to stay in business. To achieve this balance, the government sets what it deems a reasonable profit to provide the company and its investors with a sufficient rate of return. The regulators then add in all the company's expenses to arrive at a necessary level of sales. According to the number of customers and their usages, regulators set a base rate to produce the desired revenues, and thus, profit.

✔ **They rarely go out of business.** Utilities have a large captive clientele. Nearly every citizen and business needs to use their services. If a customer doesn't want to get cut off from the utility's services, he or she has to pay the bill, which means utilities can count on consistent revenues and cash flow. Unless a utility takes on extremely risky ventures, it's almost guaranteed to be profitable.

✔ **They typically pay out a large part of their earnings in dividends.** Because all their expenses are factored into the formula for determining the utility's profit, utilities have little need to reinvest profits into the business. With a lot of cash and limited potential for seeing the stock's price rise by a large amount, utilities pay out 60 to 80 percent of their annual earnings to shareholders. The typical return on shareholder equity is 10 to 12 percent.

✔ **They enjoy such steady and predictable cash flows that they rarely cut dividends.** In fact, profits and cash flow are large enough to allow the companies to hike their dividends on a regular basis. When evaluating their dividend growth, look for consistent increases that keep pace with the rate of inflation.

Potential pitfalls of utilities

Although utilities produce a lot of cash and are almost guaranteed a profit, not all of them are great investments. Here are few risks to watch out for with utilities:

✔ **Outside factors in the economy:** Increased competition, as well as the prices and supplies of raw materials (such as coal, natural gas, and water), can affect profits.

✔ **The tightening of regulation:** Increasing regulation remains the major issue for utilities. Regulators setting the base rate can decide not to allow utilities to pass certain expenses or investment costs on to the consumer. The utility and its shareholders have to bear these costs, cutting into expected profits. Smaller profit means smaller dividends. Utilities also have to deal with local and federal environmental regulations, which can increase the cost of doing business.

✔ **High debt levels:** Utilities have a lot of debt because of all the capital projects they take on. A company with a lot of debt is very susceptible to the affects of interest rates. Rising interest rates increase the company's costs by making borrowing money more expensive.

How utilities beat the market

Although utilities, like most of the stock market, took a beating during the most recent economic slump, they managed to outperform the broader market over the ten-year period of 1999 to 2008. The Dow Jones Utility Average, an index of 15 of the largest U.S. utilities, beat the Dow Jones Industrial Average, the benchmark for the broad market, in cumulative return (18.72 percent versus –4.41 percent) and *annualized* (shorter period computed as if for a whole year) returns (1.73 percent versus –0.45 percent) on both a price return and total return basis. *Price return* measures returns only in capital appreciation, and total return combines capital appreciation with income or interest.

Even more striking is that on a total return basis, which included reinvesting dividends, the Dow Jones Utilities posted a cumulative return of 70.63 percent over the ten-year period versus 17.95 percent for the Dow Jones Industrials. Annualized, that came to 5.49 percent a year for the utilities versus 1.66 percent for the industrials.

Factoring in the financial crisis, utilities still did very well. For the three years ending December 31, 2008, utility mutual funds slipped just 0.2 percent. Comparatively, the three-year annualized return of the S&P 500 was –8.36 percent.

Assessing Utility Companies: What to Look For

So how can you know which utilities *are* good investments? Following is a list of characteristics to examine when evaluating a utility for your dividend portfolio:

✔ **Dividend performance:** In most cases, you don't realize big returns from share price appreciation, so make sure the utility has been increasing its dividend payouts regularly over the last four to five years. These stocks may be rare; Josh Peters, the editor of Internet newsletter *Morningstar DividendInvestor,* says dividend cuts among utilities are "downright commonplace relative to banks or energy master limited partnerships."

Don't worry about cuts that happened at least five years ago if dividends have been growing since then, but make sure you understand the reasons for them. Were they due to poor investments, excessive debt, or poor relations with regulators? Recent cutbacks in dividends are enough to knock them out of a portfolio. If it's a small cut, you may want to stay, but for me a dividend cut is a deal breaker. Who knows when it will come back? If it doesn't, you're left with a stock with low expectations for share price appreciation. Sell these shares and put the cash into a firm with a growing dividend.

✔ **A focused business:** Utilities with nonutility businesses are riskier than pure utilities. These outside operations have the potential to divert capital away from dividends, hurting yields. When you look at the company's earnings press release or annual report, look for income and investment details broken out by separate units of the corporation. These units may be subsidiaries or company units involved in completely different businesses. As a dividend investor, stick with pure utilities.

✔ **Regulatory environment:** Some states have tighter regulations than others, and others, such as Texas, are more pro-business. States with laissez-faire attitudes about keeping rates affordable for customers tend to allow utilities to charge higher rates — bad for consumers, but good for shareholders. Florida, Texas, and California are utility-investor-friendly states. Do some research on the Internet to find out which other states fall into this category. Just go to a search engine and type in the type of utility (such as "electric"), the name of the state, and the words "regulatory atmosphere." The results should bring up the kind of information you need.

Although it often gets a negative rap, deregulation isn't necessarily bad. Because deregulation hasn't had its intended effects, utilities in a position to take advantage and charge more when supply is short post higher profits. This action may sound shady to customers, but it's good for shareholders.

✔ **Debt load:** Utilities often carry large amounts of debt because they own significant infrastructure that requires a lot of upkeep and upgrading. Typically, their liabilities are larger than their assets, but debt higher than 60 percent of total capital should be a red flag. These high debt loads make utilities extremely sensitive to fluctuations in interest rates: As interest rates rise and fall, so do the debt payments. Therefore, utilities perform best when interest rates are falling or remain low.

✔ **Very high yields:** Be wary of utilities with yields significantly higher than the sector average. High yields mean the company may be shelling out more than 80 percent of its profits, or the stock has been pushed very low. A low stock price may just be due to a broad bear market, but it may point to fundamental problems in the business. In addition, high dividend payouts may cause regulators to get tougher on the company and lower its rates, which can lead to a dividend cut.

Pumping Up Your Portfolio with Energy Partnerships

The major integrated oil and gas companies, 11 in all, hold the characteristics of good dividend stocks. They're mature, stable companies, typically with good management, that produce a product necessary to maintain modern civilization. The following sections show you the advantages and disadvantages of these stocks, as well as some to consider.

The benefits of energy company investing

Americans use oil in almost every facet of modern life, from heating their homes to driving their cars. All industries need energy, usually oil, to function, and many of the products used today are petroleum-based. As 2008's all-time-high oil price of $147 a barrel shows, when the price of oil goes up, so does the price of nearly everything else. Although the price per barrel has fallen significantly since then, it remains volatile and unlikely to return to previous super-low prices for several reasons:

- ✔ **Oil is a nonrenewable energy source.** As people consume oil, less is available, and the law of supply and demand naturally drives up its price.

- ✔ **Worldwide demand is increasing.** As China, India, and other countries become more industrialized, they need more oil and other sources of energy to fuel their growth.

- ✔ **Producers aren't interested in offering cheap oil.** The Organization of the Petroleum Exporting Countries, better known as OPEC, says a reasonable price range to make investing in oil infrastructure to meet growing demand worthwhile is in the $60 to $80 per barrel range.

Energy companies' negatives

Although energy companies offer some attractive advantages (see the preceding section), nothing is ever a one way street. They also have some significant negatives you need to consider; these pitfalls seem to affect the entire industry, so no one company should be hurt by them more than another:

- ✔ **Extreme volatility:** Oil in particular, and commodities in general, are volatile investments. Think about the huge swing in oil prices since 2002. From a low of $18 in 2002, the price tripled in less than three years. It then surged to $147 by the middle of 2008, only to fall back to $40 in early 2009.

The sharp drop in energy prices since 2014 has put a severe strain on energy companies' cash flows as they try to keep paying dividends while maintaining their rate of capital expenditures.

✔ **Peak oil:** Peak oil theory predicts severe oil shortages by 2030. Although that situation may be a good thing for investors, it also has the potential to radically change the industry. Some companies may do very well while others crumble.

✔ **Potential government intervention:** State-owned oil companies hold most of the world's oil and gas reserves, so the government can turn the taps on or off at any time.

✔ **Nationalization:** Many oil-producing countries are fairly poor. As the price of oil increases, they want more of the money, which may strain relations between the governments and the major oil companies. In some cases, countries have gone as far as to nationalize their oil assets, as Venezuela did to Exxon Mobil in 2007. As the price of oil rises, the idea of this nationalization happening in other countries is a real possibility.

✔ **Global unrest:** The people in the poorest oil-producing countries aren't terribly happy with the way the oil companies have polluted their local environments and treated the people in general, and protests commonly disrupt supplies.

✔ **Development of alternative energies:** Alternative energies, such as wind and solar, are expected to feed some of the demand for carbon fuels, including oil and coal. Although this shift would help the broader economy, it would also cause oil prices to fall.

✔ **Bad press:** The oil industry has been responsible for some of the worst environmental disasters and has been accused of being a major villain in global warming. This negativity may reduce demand for the company's stock, which would be bad for investors.

Exploring Master Limited Partnerships

Master limited partnerships or MLPs are securities that trade just like equities. But because MLPs are partnerships, not corporations, they don't sell shares or have shareholders. Rather, they sell *units* and refer to investors as *unit holders* or *partners*. The main advantage of this business structure is that the company itself avoids paying taxes, which offers enormous advantages to the dividend investor for maximizing returns. Instead, the tax liability passes directly to the individual partners based proportionally on their unit holdings.

Not all companies can claim MLP status. To qualify, a company must receive at least 90 percent of its income from interest, dividends, real estate rents, gain from the sale or disposition of real property, income and gain from commodities or commodity futures, and income and gain from activities related to minerals or natural resources.

A huge majority of MLPs are in the energy industry, but energy MLPs aren't tied so much to the price of oil and gas like other energy stocks can be. MLP companies are typically more involved in the extraction, transportation, and storage of oil and gas, so they're less affected by fluctuations in the price of crude oil.

At one time, real estate investment trusts, or REITs, held the majority of high yielding stocks, but the bursting of the housing bubble ended that run. For income investors, MLPs are the new REITs. Chapter 5 gives you more on REITs.

Although MLPs are partnerships, they aren't like energy partnerships of the 1970s and 1980s that were sold as tax shelters and many of which were scams. MLPs are legitimate vehicles that offer real tax savings.

MLP's advantages

MLPs offer a host of advantages that reach beyond the advantages offered by dividend stocks. The primary advantages include the following:

✔ **Predictable cash flows:** The MLP business structure favors the kinds of companies that create safe, steady cash flow streams — one of the most important characteristics a dividend investor should be looking for.

✔ **Distributions taxed only once:** One of the big criticisms of dividend investing is that profits are taxed twice, once at the corporate level and again on the investor's income taxes. The partnership structure eliminates one level. Like a mutual fund, the taxable profits pass through the corporate entity directly to the investors, who are responsible for the taxes.

I hear you moaning, "Oh great, I'm still stuck paying taxes on this money." Well, you were paying taxes on your dividends anyway. Because the MLP doesn't pay taxes, you receive a bigger distribution. However, MLP dividends are taxed differently than the maximum 15-percent tax on regular dividends. The following section gives you additional information about tax issues related to MLPs.

✔ **Huge yields:** In exchange for not being charged taxes, most MLPs are required to pay out all their cash flow to investors. In addition to resulting in huge cash payouts, this setup means management has very little discretion on how much to pay out or whether to cut the dividend.

✔ **Higher returns on equity:** The absence of retained cash means managers are forced to go outside the company to find funding for large capital projects. The scrutiny of outside lenders typically prevents the funding of dubious projects that follow the latest fad.

✔ **Less volatility than regular energy stocks:** Changes in energy prices typically have less effect on the price of these stocks.

✔ **Enormous potential for price appreciation:** On top of the high yields, many MLPs are growing by building new assets and acquiring competition. According to the MSN Money website, "You can think of MLPs as a pure play on the growth in demand for energy without having to worry about whether crude oil is going to $30 or $100."

MLP's disadvantages

MLPs aren't without some potential disadvantages:

✓ **Investors have little voice in company decisions.** MLPs have two classes of equity investors: general partners and limited partners. *General partners* are basically company management; they control and run the business. *Limited partners* are like shareholders; they provide the investible capital but have little say over how it's used.

✓ **Limited partners receive less when distributions are raised.** When the MLP increases distributions, the general partners stand to earn a bigger share of the increase. On the flip side, general partners suffer a bigger decrease when the MLP reduces distributions.

✓ **Partnerships bring greater liability.** Corporations are structured to remove liability from the individual owners, but in a partnership, the partners are liable in most lawsuits. Most of the time, the general partners are fully liable for legal and tax problems. Limited partners do have limited liability in that creditors can demand the return of cash distributions made to the unit holders if the liability in question arose before the distribution was paid, such as in management fraud.

✓ **The tax issues are potentially complex.** Tax issues are the major drawback of MLPs for most investors. Each unit holder must pay his or her share of the partnership's income taxes, and if you own a large enough stake in the MLP, you may have to file returns in each state in which the partnership does business. In addition, you may not be able to defer taxes by holding units in a retirement account such as an IRA. For more about tax considerations for investing, head to Chapter 11.

Qualifying companies

In 1986, tax laws changed to promote investment in *midstream* energy assets (infrastructure companies and businesses involved in extracting, processing, transporting, and storing natural resources). These natural resources include crude oil, natural gas, coal, and refined products, such as fuel oil and natural-gas liquids.

Obviously, extracting is the riskiest venture. Oil companies invest a lot of money in pinpointing potential oil reserves, securing rights to the land, drilling the well, and erecting an oil rig. If they drill in the wrong spot, they end up spending a lot of money for nothing more than a big hole in the ground. In addition, as soon as they start pumping the oil, they must contend with the fluctuations in the price of the commodity.

Transportation (pipelines) and storage, however, are two areas in the energy sector that provide a steady cash flow from which to pay unit holders. The following sections explore these two industries in greater depth.

Pipelines

Pipelines transport oil or gas from the well to wherever folks are waiting to process and use it. Due to the nature of the business, pipelines offer investors several unique advantages:

- ✔ **Pipelines establish legal regional monopolies.** Because the cost of transporting energy by truck or train can't compete with a pipeline, the only real competition comes from another pipeline following the same route. This situation rarely happens because local municipalities typically grant franchise rights allowing a single distributor to operate in the area. The inability to easily obtain a pipeline right-of-way creates a huge barrier to entry into this market for other companies wanting to compete.

- ✔ **Volatile energy prices have little effect.** Pipelines charge oil production companies a fixed fee for the volume of oil or natural gas they actually move. Some of these rates are federally regulated with generous inflation adjustments. Although the current price you can buy or sell oil for may move, the demand for oil fluctuates in a pretty narrow range. Most pipeline arrangements are long-term contracts that guarantee a certain carrying capacity. Some require payment even if the capacity isn't used.

- ✔ **Pipelines own long-lasting, high-value physical assets.** These companies hold or are building the hard assets for the U.S. energy infrastructure of the future. According to industry estimates, over the next decade, the sectors for natural gas and for crude oil and refined petroleum products will each need $100 billion in new infrastructure for processing, storage, and transportation, which means there is huge potential for growth in the pipeline industry.

✔ **Pipeline companies are growing organically.** By laying more pipeline themselves or buying other assets, pipe-line companies tend to follow a natural growth pattern. By making these acquisitions, the pipelines continue to generate strong cash flow, increasing their distributable cash flow and hence, payments to unit holders.

✔ **Maintenance costs are small.** After the pipeline's instal-lation into the ground, the annual maintenance costs are just a fraction of the operating cash flow.

Terminal and storage facilities

Pipelines are the most popular MLPs, but *terminal and stor-age facilities* (companies maintain storage tanks near pipeline systems to hold the products until transport) are also attrac-tive. They're not monopolies, but they generate stable cash flows and good returns. Revenues come from fees charged for short-term and long-term storage of the petroleum products.

Energy producers

Although the MLPs were created for hard-asset companies, many energy exploration and production firms have begun to put their assets into MLPs to avoid taxes. Like other MLPs, all their cash flow gets distributed to their unit holders, but because these firms are much more susceptible to the volatile price swings in the commodities they produce, those cash flows aren't always stable. Better-managed firms use a lot of hedges to minimize the effects of fluctuating commodity prices.

These firms buy proven long-life assets that will consistently pump out oil and gas to provide steady cash flow over time. However, wells can run dry. These firms may provide a higher yield than the pipelines, but they also carry more risk in that their income isn't fixed the way that it is for the traditional pipeline firms.

MLP stocks

Because MLPs aren't your standard, everyday dividend stocks, the same criteria may not apply to the same degree during your evaluation. With MLP stocks, take a close look at the following:

✔ **Coverage ratio:** You want the distribution of cash flow to dividend payout ratio to be higher than 1 (and the higher the better). If you see a coverage ratio of 1.25, the MLP is more likely to increase the dividends, which can push the share price higher.

✔ **Debt:** The typical MLP holds a capital structure of 50 percent debt and 50 percent equity capital. A debt level much higher than that can hurt cash flows and the payout ratio.

✔ **Changes in the tax laws:** Changes that increase the tax burden for the MLP or unit holders may have a huge affect on the yields.

✔ **Changes in the regulatory structure:** In a more tightly regulated environment, profits (and payments to unit holders) may suffer if regulators restrict how much the MLPs may charge.

✔ **Falling demand:** Although some MLPs are somewhat insulated from fluctuating commodity prices, increasing prices or an economic slowdown can hurt long-term demand and ripple through the industry.

✔ **The inability to fund new capital projects or acquisitions:** Because MLPs pass profits to unit holders, they usually need to secure outside financing to fund new projects or acquisitions. If they can't secure financing, growth and profits may stagnate.

✔ **A proliferation of alternative energy sources:** Demand for cleaner or alternative energies coupled with breakthroughs in energy technology may decrease demand for oil and reduce profits for oil companies and related industries.

Exploring Telecommunications Stocks

Prior to 1984, AT&T was the largest company in the world. With few exceptions, AT&T and its subsidiaries monopolized the entire U.S. telephone market. The federal government regulated it as a utility and, like a utility, AT&T consistently paid out dividends, even during the Great Depression. It was one of the famed "widows and orphans" stocks, so called because they were safe investments and reliable at generating income.

As part of the settlement of the antitrust lawsuit, AT&T rid itself of its local telephone service companies (the Regional Bell Operating Companies, better known as the RBOCs or "Baby Bells") and remained a provider of long-distance telephone service. The breakup led to increased competition in the long-distance area of the market with companies such as Sprint and MCI. Later, AT&T spun off its famous research company Bell Labs, renaming it Lucent Technologies, which became a huge player in the telecom equipment world.

As new industries such as cable television and the Internet sprouted up, they wanted to use the existing telephone infrastructure. The Telecommunications Act of 1996 performed a complete overhaul on the 62-year-old Communications Act of 1934 and sparked a wave of innovation that has led to the growth of cellphones, the Internet, the cable industry, fiber optics, and broadband.

The advantages

Despite the competition, the telecom industry is experiencing huge growth as more people use more of its services. It remains worthy of your interest because many telecom companies currently offer great dividends.

Companies can create steady revenue streams by locking in subscribers to one- or two-year contracts. This allows the telecoms to project their future earnings with more accuracy and provide better profit potential.

The disadvantages

The rapid pace of technological change and increased competition has made telecom stocks riskier than ever before. Two terms I associate with dividend stocks — *safe earnings* and *reliable cash flows* — no longer apply to telecom stocks because dramatic cost cutting seems to be the common strategy, and customer loyalty appears to be a relic of the past.

In addition, evaluating a telecom investment today demands much more research into the structure of the company's business model and financials than years ago, when nearly every Baby Bell company was a good investment.

Which companies qualify

So many different industries use the modern-day telecommunication industry's infrastructure that the lines defining what is and isn't a form of telecommunications have become very blurry. Some of the subsectors that qualify as telecoms are

- ✔ **Wireless companies:** As people give up their home telephones for cellphones, the wireless phone companies chip away at the classic landline telephone business. With mobile phones capable of browsing the Internet and receiving television signals, wireless companies now offer those services, grabbing advertising dollars that used to go to those other industries.

- ✔ **Cable companies:** Cable companies now offer phone services on the broadband Internet they send over their high-speed video networks.

- ✔ **Classic telephone companies:** Unwilling to sit back and do nothing, traditional phone companies offer bundled packages combining landlines with wireless services such as cellphones, the Internet, and digital TV.

- ✔ **Telecom equipment manufacturers:** Although these companies provide equipment and services to the telecom industry, they share more characteristics with technology companies than they do with the telecoms. Much less stable and with less predictable cash flows, few of these companies offer dividends. Those that do typically have yields small enough that you can ignore them.

Sector risk

Although the telecom industry features plenty of good companies for dividend investors, the sector isn't risk-free. Prior to investing, consider the following:

- ✔ **Pricing reflects intense competition.** Although companies can offer noticeable differences in service, such as the quality of the calls and networks, for the most part, telecom services all offer nearly the same thing, which means price is often the factor that determines which company a customer uses. Hence, as the cost to provide the service gets cheaper, the firms continue to lower their prices to grab subscribers from their competitors. This shift has led to the growth of the voice-over-Internet providers, who sell telephone service at about half the price of landlines. Lower prices are great if you're a customer buying a phone or new service, but investors hate price cuts because they tend to lower revenues and earnings.

✔ **Survival requires innovation.** Cellphones and smart-phones are some of the most sophisticated technology around. They not only provide a way to communicate by voice but also have become mobile entertainment systems and therefore status symbols. Most customers want access to the top-of-the-line, state-of-the-art services and products, and if a company can't provide that, customers quickly go elsewhere. Thus, companies constantly spend huge amounts of money to install and update networks, build new towers, and increase capacity all in the effort to deliver faster and clearer voice, video, and data streams. They usually take on debt to achieve these goals; high debt loads demand a steady cash stream to make interest payments and leave a company highly exposed to interest rate risk.

✔ **Regulators remain a challenge.** The telecom sector is no longer heavily regulated like a utility and has to deal with new competition, but it is still subject to federal regulations. Governments in the United States and elsewhere have a vested interest in making sure the telecommunications industry remains healthy. The U.S. Federal Communications Commission (FCC) and the European Commission in the European Union still need to approve all big mergers and acquisitions in the industry. If the regulators don't like the deal, it doesn't happen.

Assessing Telecom Stocks: What to Look For

Though telecoms still see steady cash flows from subscriber bases and have boosted dividends, the constantly changing nature of the industry leaves the stability of these businesses much more suspect than in the past. Close analysis of earnings growth, free cash flow, and the payout ratio become absolutely critical; see Chapter 8 for more about analyzing cash flow and payout ratio.

The key factors you want to look at are the company's ability to acquire and keep customers, generate revenue from those customers through a variety of services, keep costs down, and increase profitability, as I explain in the following sections.

Subscriber growth

Unlike most other industries, subscriber growth is a crucial metric for valuing a telecom company. Telecom customers are called *subscribers* because many sign up for service for an extended period of time. The more subscribers a company has, the stronger the company's revenue stream and the greater potential for profit growth. By locking in subscribers to one- or two-year contracts, telecoms can project their future earnings with more accuracy.

Because this number is of much interest to investors, telecoms report the change in their subscriber base, either up or down, in their quarterly earnings reports. The formula is pretty simple:

Growth Rate = New Subscribers ÷ Total Subscribers at beginning of period

If the company with 200,000 subscribers at the beginning of the quarter signed 2,800 new subscribers during the quarter, it would post a growth rate of 1.4 percent:

2,800 New Subscribers ÷ 200,000 Total Subscribers = 1.4 percent Growth Rate

You want to see a growth rate rising. A flattening or falling growth rate may mean the company has lost its competitive edge.

Customer base and churn rate

The *churn rate* is a ratio that measures the percentage of subscribers who discontinue their service during a specific time period. Here's the equation:

$$\text{Churn Rate} = \text{Canceled Subscriptions} \div \text{Total Subscribers at Beginning of the Period}$$

If 4,200 subscribers out of a possible 200,000 quit, the churn rate is

$$4,200 \div 200,000 = 2.1 \text{ percent}$$

Because customers can easily switch providers and take their phone number with them, the providers of landlines and wireless phone services exist in an intensely competitive market where an increase in prices or poor service can have immediate effects. You want to see a low churn rate.

In order to grow, the company's growth rate of new subscribers must exceed the churn rate. A company with a churn rate of 2.1 percent and a 1.4 percent growth rate is losing a third more subscribers than it brings in. This deficit will likely affect revenues and earnings this quarter. If the churn rate keeps rising, the churn is likely the result of poor service and may be the sign to sell.

Average revenue per user

Average revenue per user (ARPU) is the key indicator of how the actual business of providing telecom services is performing. It measures the average monthly or quarterly revenue generated from each customer. Typically, a company breaks out each revenue stream, such as cellphone service, Internet, and downloads, and calculates total change in dollars. A company can much more easily sell new services to existing clients because it knows exactly where they are and what they like. For instance, if you buy a monthly cellphone service, and the company increases your number of minutes or offers a bundled package of music downloads, game subscriptions, and video streaming, it can increase revenues with minimal costs. Telecoms also try to raise ARPU numbers by targeting customers who want to cut down on the number of bills, encouraging them to buy as many services as they can from one company.

Companies that rely on outdated services are likely to see falling ARPUs, but a company with a foot firmly planted in popular technology has stronger prospects. For instance, many providers of telephone services experienced declining revenues in their landline business as subscribers gave up their home phones and exclusively used their mobile phones. On the other end, when Apple came out with its highly coveted iPhone, it gave AT&T an exclusive contract for providing the phone's wireless services. Anyone who wanted an iPhone was forced to sign up with AT&T even if they didn't like the service. As more people bought iPhones, AT&T sold more Internet services and applications to subscribers, increasing its ARPU. However, when Apple let other telecoms serve the iPhone, AT&T's ARPU fell as subscribers defected.

Watch out when the number of subscribers rises but revenues sink or even remain steady. This situation may indicate that the company cut prices to gain customers without increasing revenue — a key warning sign.

Consolidation

As telecoms compete by cutting prices, they need to become more efficient to maintain profitability. One way is through *economies of scale,* a situation in which fixed costs are spread over a large group as more goods are produced or services provided. This system actually lowers the average cost of producing each unit and is especially helpful to companies with wide geographic reach, giving a telecom the incentive to buy up competitors. In addition, mergers eliminate competitors, lessening the pricing pressure on a company and maybe even initiating a price hike.

EBITDA

To expand and maintain their services, telecoms must continually invest in their networks of fiber optics and towers. Don't be surprised to see an otherwise healthy company post a net loss on its income statement if it spends a lot on capital expenditures (CapEx) or the interest payments to fund that

CapEx. Companies in the cable and telecom industries typically have high debt levels and huge interest costs, which can make posting a true profit very difficult.

Because high interest expenses and taxes can decimate a company's profits, carefully examine the company's Earnings Before Interest, Taxation, Depreciation, and Amortization (EBITDA). *EBITDA* (often pronounced *ee*-bit-dah) provides a way to evaluate the operations of the core business before these costs and CapEx are taken out. Wall Street analysts look at EBITDA because it gives them an objective way to compare the profitability of highly leveraged companies in capital-intensive industries.

To calculate a company's EBITDA for yourself, use the following calculation (get the numbers from the company's quarterly reports as Chapter 8 explains):

$$\text{EBITDA} = \text{Net Income} + \text{Interest} + \text{Taxes} + \text{Depreciation} + \text{Amortization}$$

Unlike Net Income, EBITDA has no specific Generally Accepted Accounting Principles (GAAP), which means the numbers you get to figure EBITDA can be much more easily manipulated.

Debt versus equity

Spending to maintain and expand their networks is basic operating procedure at telecoms, and you don't want to ignore these expenditures, especially the amount of debt they take on to finance these new projects. Although debt can be very helpful in growing a business, relying on debt too much to finance operations can produce serious problems — in particular, large interest payments and an inability to weather bad economic conditions.

To assess a company's health in terms of debt and equity, calculate the debt-to-equity ratio:

$$\text{Debt-to-Equity Ratio} = \text{Total Liabilities} \div \text{Shareholders' Equity}$$

Too much debt can mean less cash for dividends and may even lead to dividend cuts. Lower is better, but too low means the company may be ignoring growth opportunities to avoid taking on debt. You want to see a debt-to-equity ratio around 1. The higher the number, the riskier (and potentially more unstable) the company.

Free cash flow

Another very helpful metric for determining the health of a telecom's dividend is *free cash flow* (FCF). The variables for FCF come from the cash flow statement, which looks at the money moving in and out of the company, including capital expenditures. Chapter 8 gives you more info on FCF and the cash flow statement, but for now you can use the following formula to calculate it:

Free Cash Flow = Net Cash from Operating Activities – Capital Expenditures

You want to see free cash flow large enough to cover both the interest payments on the debt and the dividend. In general, after determining the FCF, you want to look at the following two ratios:

- ✔ **Interest Ratio = Free Cash Flow + Interest Payments:** You want to see free cash flow at least double the interest payments (a ratio of 2). Too low, and it may affect the dividend's stability. Less than 1, and the company isn't even generating enough cash to cover its interest payments.

- ✔ **Payout Ratio = Dividends per Share + Earnings per Share:** For the telecom industry, a payout ratio below 60 percent is ideal because the company still needs to reinvest profits in building and maintaining infrastructure. Be careful if it exceeds a payout ratio of 75 percent because it indicates the company will need to take on much more debt to finance projects.

Discovering the Consumer Goods Sector

When it comes to human beings, you can count on one thing: They consume stuff. People need all sorts of products to live, including food, beverages, personal hygiene and cleaning products, and even technically nonessential items that some people can't live without, such as coffee, cigarettes, and alcohol. In addition, people *want* all sorts of stuff to feel comfortable and make their lives more enjoyable: electronics, appliances, new cars, restaurant meals, and more.

The good thing for consumer goods investors is that consumers always use up what they buy and need more. In the following sections, I introduce the two types of consumer goods companies, reveal why companies of the second type are typically better for dividend investors, and then explain what makes these companies potentially such good picks.

What is a consumer goods company?

Any company that manufactures or distributes products that people use falls into the consumer goods category, but this category includes two subcategories: consumer cyclicals and consumer staples.

Consumer cyclicals

Consumer cyclicals owe their name to the fact that demand for these products waxes and wanes, typically in lock step with the economy. Products in this category fall into two categories: durable and nondurable goods.

- ✔ **Durable goods** are physical goods that should last for years, such as cars, electronics, hardware, and appliances.

- ✔ **Nondurable goods** represent services and less-tangible items, such as anything related to entertainment or travel, including movies, concerts, air travel, hotels, and restaurants.

The share prices of cyclical stocks correlate to the movement of the business cycle and consumer sentiment regarding the economy. During a boom, these companies see strong sales and profits as retail and leisure spending increases. People have plenty of disposable income or are confident enough to borrow the money to pay for these creature comforts. When times aren't so good, consumers tighten their budgets, and these products are the first items to get squeezed out, because they aren't necessary. On top of being poor buy-and-hold stocks, cyclicals make poor dividend stocks because the volatility of their earnings leads to unreliable cash flow, which can lead to dividend cuts.

Consumer staples

Consumer staples are noncyclical: No matter which part of the business cycle the market is in, demand for these products doesn't slow down. Consumer staples have a low correlation to the gyrations of the stock market because people need to buy these items to carry on their everyday lives. (Utilities are another classic noncyclical sector.)

Because consumer staples are must-have products compared to the want-to-have nature of cyclicals, they exhibit most of the essential characteristics for a dividend stock:

- Mature companies
- Effective management
- Stability
- Steady stream of income
- Predictable cash flow

Most consumer staples fall under the heading of *consumables,* also referred to as *consumer-packaged goods* (CPG). These packaged products get consumed quickly and need to be replaced on a steady schedule. Even during a recession, people need to eat, bathe, and brush their teeth every day. Consumers' constant need for consumables provides these companies with steady sales and predictable cash flow, which translates into a stock that doesn't fall much during market corrections and is great to own during economic downturns.

Not only do consumer staples have limited volatility in share price, but they also have less risk than the general market and provide nice-sized yields. Although high yield often means little capital appreciation, some staples have the potential to grow two to three times the rate of inflation. Typically, consumer staples post middle-range yields higher than the S&P 500 average.

Many investors find these companies too boring to invest in because the flip side of low risk of loss is that they don't see big gains when the stock market surges. This low correlation of share prices to the swings in the market puts consumer staples in the category of *defensive stocks,* so named because they defend the portfolio from the market's fluctuations. Defensive stocks provide steady earnings and predictable cash flows that allow a company to maintain the dividend during bad times and increase it when conditions improve.

The low correlation of defensive stocks to the movements of the broader market means their share prices may rise while the market falls or plateaus.

What influences a consumer staple's income?

With a steady demand for their products in good times and bad and a lot of competition, companies in the consumer staples industry have a difficult time increasing profits and dividend payments through rising demand or increasing prices. However, they do produce steady earnings growth. They just need to be more creative in differentiating their products from their competitors. For foods and beverages, taste is a great way to stand out from rivals, but what about soap and shampoo? Here the companies rely on branding, advertising, marketing, and good-old cost- and price-cutting to attract attention to their products.

Brand strength

Branding is a strategy companies use to create differences between products that are very similar in quality. Strictly speaking, brand is the name and packaging of the product. But the concept of brand is essentially a feeling about the qualities the consumer associates with the product.

Sometimes brands have qualities, such as taste, that truly differentiate them from competitors. Heinz Ketchup and Hunt's Catsup are both a type of sweetened tomato sauce, yet their recipes are distinct enough that a person who likes the taste of one may not like the taste of the other. Coke versus Pepsi is another good example.

However, some brands are more a feeling or perception than any real difference, so companies use advertising and promotions to build and boost their brands. Is one laundry detergent really better than any other, or do consumers merely think it's better because of the way it's been marketed? Companies hope their marketing strategies will keep customers coming back to their products out of *brand loyalty.*

Because brand strength relies so much on how consumers *feel* about the brand, it may be tough to pin down, but you can gauge brand strength by looking at a company's *market share,* which is the percentage of the market the brand owns:

Market Share = Product's Revenue ÷ Total Revenue from Sales of All Products in the Same Market

Market share provides a good indicator for how well a product is doing against its competitors. For instance, if Laundry Detergent A posts sales of $6 million a year and the total market is $200 million, Detergent A's market share is 3 percent. If Laundry Detergent B posts sales of $10 million, Detergent B owns 5 percent of the market, indicating that more consumers prefer Detergent B to Detergent A.

Unfortunately, market share is a tricky number and isn't easy to find. Not all companies break out the sales of individual markets, so getting a feel for how much money is being spent in any broad market may be difficult. The easiest way to get a market share for a company or a product is from a Wall Street analyst's report. However, you typically need to be a client of the firm. You can check industry publications, *AdWeek* magazine, or articles on Yahoo! Finance and Google Finance, which may include market share estimates.

Cost cutting

One way to boost profits and lift share prices is to reduce the cost of business, especially with the materials needed to make the products. Most of the materials to create consumer goods are commodities — wherever you buy them, the quality is pretty much the same. Companies can reduce their cost of materials by switching suppliers, merging with or buying suppliers, buying larger quantities for discounts, and leveraging the *economies of scale* (the spreading of fixed costs over a large group) that come from good management.

Price reductions

When looking at consumer staples, make sure their pricing is stable or growing. You don't want a company that may have to lower prices to keep up with the competition or raise prices because of rising material costs. Both situations cut into profit margins. However, don't write off a price cut right away. Because the products a staple sells are very similar to its rival, one company may lower prices as a way to boost profits and expand market share by grabbing new customers.

Identifying a Good Consumer Staples Stock

Consumer staples include a lot of companies producing very similar products. But just because these are mature companies doesn't mean they don't need to keep growing sales and profits at least as fast as the country's general population. As you evaluate companies in this sector, look for management that's successful at maintaining or lowering the costs of goods sold while increasing sales and revenue.

A key sign of growth at a consumer staple is an operating margin that continues to rise. The operating margin measures the efficiency of a company's pricing strategy by seeing the profits before interest and taxes are paid. The *operating margin* is the percentage of revenue that remains from the sale of a product after subtracting the variable costs of producing that product, including the cost of wages and raw materials:

Operating Margin = Operating Income ÷ Net Sales

Operating margins vary from industry to industry, but in general, look for operating margins in the mid-to-high teens.

A company can raise its margins in numerous ways. Here are two of the most commonly used methods

- ✔ **Add new benefits to an existing product (increasing its value) and raise the price.** Because the company doesn't have to spend so much on developing an entirely new product, it can boost its profit without significantly increasing the cost of producing the product.

- ✔ **Add a new product line.** If the company can launch a new product line by using, for the most part, the personnel and equipment it already has, it can do so cost-effectively.

When evaluating operating margins, determine whether the sales growth is from more sales or fewer sales at higher prices. You want to avoid a situation in which the company is raising prices as sales and market share decline.

Also check how much the company spends on research and development and on sales and promotions. Did it boost margins but cut its budgets for research and advertising, or did it become more cost efficient, leading it to continue to invest in R&D, ads, and promotions?

In addition to carefully evaluating a company's operating margin, look for the following positive signs:

- ✔ **Innovation:** The launch of new products creates new revenue streams and gives the company a competitive edge until rivals begin to enter the new market.

- ✔ **A high barrier to entering the market:** The *barrier to entering a market* indicates how easily competing firms and products can enter the market. A low barrier means this entry is pretty easy; because most consumer products are easy to replicate, these markets have low barriers to entry and most brands have a lot in common with their competitors. Look for companies whose products have a barrier to others entering the same market.

- ✔ **Access to international markets:** Selling products to international markets enables a company to continue growing sales even if the local market is in a downturn.

✔ **Better treatment at stores:** Although evaluating how effectively a company gets its products to its customers is difficult, you can gain insight into the company's relationships with its retailers by doing your own field research. The more powerful brands get better treatment and more attention at a retailer because of a strong brand–retailer relationship, which is a sign of competitive strength. Usually, the powerful products sit at the front of aisles, or on shelves at eye level.

Chapter 5

Exploring REITs and Financials

*R*EITs and financials comprise a short list of what many experts deem the has-beens of dividend stock investing. The popping of the housing bubble over 2006 and 2007 blew away the REITs. The ensuing financial crisis shook the foundation of the financial industry, including many large banks, and led to widespread dividend cuts in both industries. Some banks even eliminated their dividends.

Amid the carnage remained a small but strong group of dividend providers in both industries. These survivors managed to weather the storm and capitalized on the crisis as their competitors fell out of contention. For instance, a REIT's ability to continue paying a stable dividend in the wake of the bursting housing bubble says something about the resilience of its properties and its management's expertise. Of course, a REIT that pays a sizeable dividend and has a solid cash flow isn't a sure thing, but it's certainly worthy of consideration.

This chapter explores some hard-hit industries traditionally considered fertile ground for dividend investors and provides guidance on how to identify the top picks in each sector.

REIT Basics

Real estate investment trusts, or REITs, provide a way for investors to receive capital appreciation and income from real estate without having to actually purchase and maintain property. It's like being an owner/landlord without all the hassles and responsibilities that typically accompany those roles. True to their name, REITs are trusts, not corporations. Like any trust, a REIT has beneficiaries: the shareholders.

To be considered a REIT, these trusts must follow the requirements of the Real Estate Investment Trust Act of 1960. This law states that if the trusts follow certain criteria, they're exempt from paying corporate income tax and capital gains taxes. The main criterion? The trust needs to pay out at least 90 percent of its annual profit to shareholders. This huge payout typically results in high yields. I discuss the other criteria in "Which companies qualify" later in this chapter.

REITs trade like stocks but in some ways are more like mutual funds. Like stocks, shares of a REIT

- ✔ Trade publicly on a stock exchange and are bought and sold through a stockbroker.
- ✔ Are sold in an initial public offering (IPO).
- ✔ Are very liquid. You can buy and sell them anytime the stock market is open for business.
- ✔ Have the same trading options as stocks, including short sales and limit orders.
- ✔ Pay dividends to investors.
- ✔ Are subject to SEC regulations and carry the same SEC reporting requirements as stocks.

Like a mutual fund, a REIT is

- ✔ An investment company that manages investment assets instead of selling goods and services. A REIT buys, rents, leases, manages, develops, and sells buildings — commercial, industrial, or residential developments. The REIT is typically a landlord, generating revenue from rents, property leases, and fees. REITS may also earn interest from mortgages they own. In addition, the underlying assets can increase in property value.

✔ A pool of money accumulated from many investors looking for a diversified real estate investment portfolio.

✔ A portfolio run by a professional manager.

✔ A portfolio that holds assets that it can sell off if it needs to be liquidated.

✔ A tax entity that helps investors avoid double-taxation. Trusts, like mutual funds, don't pay taxes. The tax expense is passed onto, and becomes a liability of, the shareholder.

In the following sections, I reveal some of the advantages and disadvantages of investing in REITs and explain which companies qualify as REITs.

The pros and cons

When you buy a REIT, you're becoming more of a real estate investor than a dividend stock investor. This move carries some advantages and disadvantages, which I discuss in the following sections.

Advantages

A REIT offers several advantages to both stock and real estate investors:

✔ **REITs must pay out at least 90 percent of their income as dividends.** This requirement is the number one reason why investors buy REITs. Management can raise the payout to more than 90 percent but, by law, can't lower it below 90 percent. In other words, management can't decide to slash the dividend payment.

✔ **Large payouts result in higher-than-average yields.** For dividend investors, high yield is a primary consideration.

✔ **REITs help diversify an investment portfolio.** Because real estate values don't generally correlate to stock prices, stock prices and real estate values can move together or in completely opposite directions. Unless a real estate slump triggers a financial crisis or vice versa, a portfolio that contains both stock and real estate holdings may provide some protection over slumps that affect only one or the other.

✔ **REITs help diversify a real estate portfolio.** Money pooled from many investors allows the trust to purchase more buildings than an individual would be able to buy alone. If you buy real estate on your own, you may lock up all your money in one building. A REIT gives you a piece of many different properties. That way, one under-performing building won't ruin your portfolio. This setup allows small investors to have a diversified real estate portfolio with a minimal investment.

✔ **You can own real estate without the costs and hassles associated with owning physical buildings.** You don't have to find and research properties — the REIT's managers do that for you. You don't need to come up with a down payment and closing costs or worry about making monthly mortgage payments and maintaining properties. You can jump into the real estate market with a purchase as small as one share of stock.

✔ **REITs own physical assets with a value all their own that can appreciate over time.** As an investor, you own tangible assets that tend to rise in value over the long term.

✔ **REITs are more liquid than typical real estate investments.** Selling property is a long, time-consuming process. With REITs, you simply sell your shares on the stock market in a matter of minutes.

Disadvantages

Because REITs allow you to invest in real estate, they carry risks associated with real estate investing as well as stock investing, including the following:

✔ Falling occupancy rates and increasing vacancies hurt revenues.

✔ Share prices can drop when property values fall.

✔ Share prices can fall with the broader stock market based on supply and demand of shares.

✔ High dividend payouts for REITs force management to take on debt to expand real estate holdings.

✔ Rising interest rates hurt profitability.

✔ Not all REIT dividends qualify for 15-percent tax rates. Some are taxed as ordinary income.

Prior to investing in a REIT, consult a tax advisor to determine the net effect on your tax bill.

Which companies qualify

Just because you own a real estate stock doesn't mean it's a REIT. When you're looking at REITs, determine whether the trust receives the tax-free benefit. To avoid paying corporate income tax and capital gains taxes, the company must follow certain rules, including the following:

✔ At least 75 percent of the REIT's annual gross income must come from real-estate related income, such as rents.

✔ At least 75 percent of the REIT's total assets must be in real estate investments, such as property or loans secured by property.

✔ Shareholders must receive a minimum of 90 percent of the REIT's taxable income. The REIT pays taxes on any income it retains.

After a company agrees to satisfy all those requirements, management can focus on one of three areas: property, mortgages, or a hybrid of the two.

✔ **Property REITs** follow a classic landlord scenario. They make their money by leasing properties and collecting rent. Success hinges on management's ability to secure properties in high-rent districts and manage them effectively. It's all about location, location, location.

✔ **Mortgage REITs** operate more like banks than landlords. These companies make, own, and manage loans for the purchase of real estate. Instead of earning revenues from rent, the REIT earns interest on its loans. Often the loans are funded by money the REIT borrowed. With increased levels of interest-rate risk and credit risk, mortgage REITs are riskier than property REITs, and dividends are less stable. Many of these companies faced financial distress during the 2008–2009 financial crisis. Their dividends fell with their falling profits.

✔ As you may guess, a **hybrid REIT** is a cross between a property and a mortgage REIT. Hybrids buy, own, and manage both properties and loans, which can provide some protection against fluctuations in the real estate markets. As properties become costlier to purchase and own, the mortgage side often declines while demand for rentals rises.

Evaluating REITs

Because REITs aren't your average, everyday dividend stocks, using the criteria from Chapter 8 to evaluate them makes little sense. The following sections show you various ways you can get an idea of a REIT's condition before investing.

Assessing REITs

Determining the value of real estate assets requires a unique set of criteria. When shopping for REITs, examine the following factors:

- **Geography:** A property's value and rent-generating potential are both closely linked to the property's location. Look for REITs that invest in areas with growing populations and thriving economies. Carefully research an area before buying a REIT that invests heavily in that area.

- **Property type:** Office and industrial properties charge higher rents but tend to suffer more in a recession as occupancy rates decline when companies go out of business. Residential and retail buildings tend to charge lower rents but are more resistant to tough economic times.

- **Diversification:** Is the trust well diversified? Many REITs focus on just one sector of the market — commercial, industrial, or residential — or just one local market. Because not all real estate markets move together, diversification is a good thing.

- **Occupancy trends:** An increasing occupancy rate is a good sign. In real estate, high vacancy rates can wipe out profits. Find out the vacancy rate for the properties the REIT holds and determine the direction the vacancy rate is moving — up or down. Although a vacancy rate of more than 10 percent may affect a REITs ability to pay dividends, the trend is more important than the actual figure. Beware if vacancies are on the rise.

✔ **Tenant concentration:** Determine whether the bulk of the REIT's income comes from just one type of tenant or industry or a wider range. If the REIT invests only in gas stations or only in strip malls, its profits may be tied too closely with the health of a particular industry or location. Research not only the REIT and type of real estate it owns but also the tenant's industry.

✔ **Management:** The reputation, strength, and skill of the company's managers are at least as important as the type of building. Check for managers that have an excellent track record for picking properties with high potential for capital appreciation, purchasing them at bargain prices, and then managing the properties for maximum profitability.

✔ **Credit rating:** Because most property is bought with borrowed money, make sure the REIT has an excellent credit rating so that it can borrow money at competitive interest rates.

✔ **Lease duration:** Ask management about the average lease duration of its holdings. Single-year leases give landlords the ability to raise rents regularly but provide tenants with an easy out. Multiyear leases lock in tenants and provide a predictable revenue stream on which you can base expectations of steady dividend payments.

✔ **Funds from operations:** Perhaps the most important factor to consider is the REIT's funds from operations (FFO), which provides an indication of how much money the REIT has available to fund dividend payments. (See the following section for more about this key figure.)

Calculating funds from operations (FFO)

Net income isn't always the be-all and end-all of an entity's success, especially when looking at the entity's ability to pay dividends. Earnings per share and the P/E ratio don't give the most accurate representation of a REIT's value because the net income calculation deducts depreciation. Deducting for depreciation misrepresents the REIT's value because it takes part of the property's value out of income producing assets, even as the property continues to rise in value and produce income. A better number for evaluating the REIT's overall performance and ability to pay dividends is called *funds from operations* (FFO), which indicates how much cash is available for paying dividends:

FFO = Net Income + Depreciation – Gains from One-Time Sales

FFO is similar to net cash flow (NCF) from operating activities. Both NCF and FFO add back in depreciation and amortization because these are non-cash charges. In FFO, this add-back means the REIT has a predictable pile of tax-free cash sitting in its vault equal to the value of the depreciation and amortization, ready to pay out as dividends over the coming years.

However, there's one key difference: NCF, which deals with the actual movement of cash during the quarter, includes one-time gains and losses, but FFO doesn't. With FFO, analysts just want to see the amount of sustainable dividend-paying cash that comes strictly from operations.

Most REITs report their FFOs in press releases along with their quarterly earnings, as shown in Table 5-1. Table 5-1 is part of the earnings report of a company called Big Edifice Realty and shows you how to figure out FFO and adjusted FFO from the net income; you may then use those numbers to determine the FFO per share, the adjusted FFO per share, and the payout ratio the company's dividend represents.

Most analysts value REITs by their FFO per share:

FFO per Share = FFO ÷ Total Shares Outstanding

In Table 5-1, the REIT's net income is $26.497 million, or 29 cents per share. After adding depreciation with adjustments back in ($22,922), and then subtracting the gains from the sale of real estate ($2,239), FFO comes in much higher, at $47.18 million, or 52 cents per share.

To obtain an accurate indication of a REIT's performance, always calculate the dividend payout ratio using the FFO, not net income.

Table 5-1	Big Edifice Realty FFO		
June 30, 2009	*Net Income*	*FFO*	*Adjusted FFO*
Net income after preferred dividends	$26,497,000	$26,497,000	$26,497,000
Add in depreciation and Amortization		$22,961,000	$22,961,000
Depreciations adjustments		($39,000)	($58,000)
Subtract income from sale of real estate held for investment		($2,239,000)	($2,222,000)
Subtract capital expenditures			($593,000)
Totals	$26,497,000	$47,180,000	$46,587,000
Common stock outstanding	91,000,000 shares	91,000,000 shares	91,000,000 shares
Amount per share	29 cents	52 cents	51 cents
Payout ratio on dividend of 42.6 cents a share	147%	82%	84%

The REIT paid out dividends of 42.6 cents a share. Comparing that to net income, the payout ratio comes in at an astounding 147 percent. It's ridiculously huge and unsustainable, and it violates all the rules about dividend payouts. The REIT, however, has a stash of cash sitting in its depreciation vault. Add that cash back in when determining the FFO, and the payout ratio is 82 percent of FFO. Lower is better, and a payout ratio of 85 percent or less gives the REIT a bigger cushion to fall back on.

For a REIT to achieve tax-exempt status, it needs to pay out at least 90 percent of its taxable income, not FFO (no requirement dictates how much of the FFO must be paid to shareholders). Because FFO is typically much higher than taxable income, the dividend payout is usually a smaller percentage.

Calculating adjusted funds from operations (AFFO)

Some analysts think that the cash available for dividend payouts should take into account the cost of maintaining the buildings. If you own a home, you know buildings demand constant upkeep, such as painting and new fixtures. Analysts subtract the capital expenditures for maintaining the properties to arrive at a more conservative measurement, *adjusted funds from operations* (AFFO):

AFFO = FFO – Capital Expenditures

FFO and AFFO are *non-GAAP earnings,* which means the numbers don't adhere to Generally Accepted Accounting Principles (GAAP) — the authoritative standards by which revenue, net income, and balance sheet components must be presented in filings with the SEC. Many companies don't like GAAP earnings, because they feel the standards are too strict and fail to provide an accurate measure of the company's performance. To counteract this perceived discrepancy, companies often provide their own numbers alongside the required GAAP earnings — an alternative non-GAAP earnings measurement, such as EBITDA or FFO.

Accounting for debt

Typically, a payout ratio below 85 percent of FFO and a recurring revenue stream should give you a good indication of the dividend's stability. However, because most of a REIT's cash is paid to shareholders as dividends, little equity remains for buying properties. Thus, most REITs have high debt levels and maximize shareholder returns through leverage. In addition to the other debt ratios mentioned in Chapter 9, look at the REIT's debt-to-capital ratio.

The *debt-to-capital ratio* adds together all forms of debt (long-term and short-term) and then divides by total capital, which equals total debt plus shareholder equity (preferred stock and common stock).

Debt-to-Capital Ratio = Total Debt ÷ Total Capital

Josh Peters, editor of the *Morningstar DividendInvestor* monthly newsletter, says the debt-to-capital ratio should be less than 65 percent on a market value basis and equal to or less than 80 percent of an FFO basis. In an interview after the financial crisis, Peters told me that investors need to look not just at the total amount of debt but also when the debt comes due: Will the REIT meet its obligations on an ongoing basis or will it need to borrow money when the credit markets are difficult? Typically, a REIT pays off a loan coming due with a new loan. But when no one was lending during the 2008–2009 credit crunch, REITs saw their short-term debts come due at a time when they weren't able to secure new loans. Desperate to pay off their debt with the funds from operations, many REITs slashed their dividends, which is why dividend investors want to keep an especially close eye on this factor.

Valuing a REIT

Valuing a REIT is similar to valuing a corporation (see Chapter 9), but you use FFO per share rather than earnings per share and a P/FFO ratio rather than the P/E ratio.

FFO/share measures the company's performance from year to year and allows you to compare the performance of two companies. To calculate a company's FFO and FFO/share, see "Calculating funds from operations (FFO)" earlier in this chapter.

The P/E ratio (covered in Chapter 9) gives you a *multiple* (how much an investor pays for $1 of profit) with which to compare two companies' relative valuations. Because FFO is the main metric among REITs, use the P/FFO ratio to calculate the multiple:

P/FFO Multiple = Price per Share ÷ FFO per Share

The lower the multiple, the cheaper the stock compared to FFO. The preferred multiple varies depending on property type — commercial, residential, or industrial — and on the local real estate market. To get the multiple levels for each category, read some Wall Street research from analysts. As a rule of thumb, look for REITs with a P/FFO ratio below 10.

If you're focusing on the dividend yield much more than capital appreciation, making sure the company has a recurring cash stream for predictable payouts should be enough. If you want capital appreciation, look at growth levels.

Looking for growth among the REITs

If you're looking for capital appreciation in addition to dividends, look for the following signs of growth:

- ✔ Rent increases
- ✔ Rising occupancy rates
- ✔ Success in buying bargain properties, upgrading them, and renting them out
- ✔ The growth rate at which the company acquires new properties

To compare your REIT or REIT fund to the broader REIT market, check out the two benchmarks for the market: the MSCI U.S. REIT Index and the Dow Jones U.S. Real Estate Investment Trusts Index.

Dividends from Banks

Banks have always paid dividends, but for most of the 1990s they posted yields below 3 percent. Then, in the first decade of the new century, banks became great stocks for dividend investors by offering a great package of total return with fast earnings growth and rising payout ratios.

With the fiscal crisis of 2008, the entire banking industry blew up. Many banks went out of business, and of those that survived, many either cut their dividends or eliminated them entirely. J.P. Morgan Chase, the strongest of the bunch, cut its dividend by 87 percent in early 2009.

Many banks needed to be bailed out by the federal government. In the aftermath of the bank bailouts, with dividends and balance sheets decimated, the banking sector as a whole wasn't promising. However, many of the banks that dramatically cut their dividends during the fiscal crisis have stabilized, returned to profitability, and reinstated their dividends.

Not every bank filled its loan portfolio with loans to subprime lenders and credit default swaps. Many banks maintained a conservative business strategy. They not only survived but also came out much stronger and were able to grab market share by buying competitors. These survivors are the banks you want to put your money in. They shouldn't be too hard to find — they're the ones still paying a decent dividend. Funny how that worked out.

The pros and cons

If you're waffling about whether to invest in banks, I can give you plenty more to waffle about. In the following sections, I reveal the pros and cons to consider before deciding to invest a portion of your portfolio in banks.

Pros

In terms of stability and reliability, banks actually have a lot going for them:

- ✓ **Plentiful supply of cheap money:** Banks have a constant source of cheap funds: depositors. Most other lending institutions need to form partnerships or sell equity or debt to investors to raise the money they lend. These companies pay a premium for that money by giving away part of the company or paying interest. Not banks. Customers just hand them cash, practically for free, relying on the bank to keep their money safe and liquid. Most checking accounts pay 0 percent interest, and recently, savings accounts haven't paid much more.

- ✓ **Customer stability:** When customers choose a bank, they tend to stay put because the time, money, and hassle of changing banks typically outweigh the benefits. As soon as customers receive their checks and ATM cards and set up direct deposit and electronic bill pay, they've made a significant investment of time and are reluctant to do it all over again with another bank.

- ✓ **Stiff regulation:** Banks are a heavily regulated industry, and after the banking fiascos of 2008 and 2009, regulators are becoming even stricter in monitoring banks and enforcing regulations, which benefits investors in two ways. First, it enhances customer stability by increasing customer confidence in making deposits. Second, it helps stabilize the banking industry, so your investment is safer.

✔ **Economies of scale:** Size matters. A huge company can force suppliers to give it better, cheaper goods than competitors; it then spreads the fixed costs over a greater number of stores. By lowering its cost of doing business so much, it can still make huge profit margins while charging less than its competition. Big banks with many branches have economies of scale by spreading costs over a large network of branches.

Cons

Don't assume that investing in banks is 100-percent risk-free. Investors who owned stock in Washington Mutual learned this lesson the hard way in September 2008, when the FDIC seized Washington Mutual — a bank that held a loan portfolio with $307 billion in assets. WaMu was the largest bank failure in U.S. history. Depositors got their money back. Shareholders lost everything.

Another risk of investing in banks is, well, risk. Banks act as financial intermediaries between the people who need the money and the people who have it. As banks manage the money that flows through them, they assume two types of risk, interest rate risk and credit risk:

✔ **Interest rate risk:** Banks may pinch pennies, but sometimes they can get pinched too. More precisely, their *net interest spread* (the difference between the rate they charge on their assets and the rate they pay to their liabilities) can feel the pinch when the interest they collect on loans dips, the interest they pay on deposits rises, or both.

- Most deposits and CDs have short-term maturities, so a sudden rise in interest rates forces the bank to pay more for deposits. Unless the bank can charge more on loans, the spread tightens.

- When interest rates rise, more people may deposit money in the bank while fewer people take out loans.

- Banks can also get their money tied up in bonds — a loan with a fixed interest rate. If interest rates rise, the bond's coupon loses value compared to competing investments.

To offset a tightening of the spread, the bank may institute more fees and charges to make up the missing revenue.

The *yield curve* determines the amount of interest rate risk. It's a graph that examines bonds with the same credit quality by plotting out their yields over a range of maturities from shortest to longest. Banks like when short-term rates are low and the curve makes a steep upward move to the longer maturities, because they pay depositors short-term rates while charging borrowers long-term rates. This wide spread increases profitability. When long-term yields aren't much higher than short-term yields, the yield curve is much flatter, cutting into profits.

Depending on which assets the bank holds, net interest income can be very sensitive to changes in interest rates. Deposit accounts with short-term maturities may pay variable interest rates, which fluctuate up and down. Meanwhile, many liabilities have a fixed rate, although adjustable-rate mortgages do see rate increases.

✓ **Credit risk:** *Credit risk* is the likelihood that a bank will lose part or all of the principal, as well as the interest, in the event a borrower defaults on the loan. Poor management of credit risk was a major contributor to the fiscal crisis of 2008. Rising interest rates can hurt adjustable-rate loans because they increase the interest payments the borrowers must pay, potentially causing them to miss payments and turning these into problem loans. Banks hold cash in allowances to absorb these potential losses, but if their reserves fall short, they can get into a serious credit crunch of their own.

Financial services perform best in low interest-rate environments. When interest rates decline, banks pay depositors less interest as revenue from mortgages and loans increases. In addition, a drop in interest rates usually sparks a boost in business development, leading to more borrowing to finance new projects.

Watch out for super-low interest rates. In late 2009, interest rates in the U.S. were at historic lows. The *federal funds rate* (the rate banks charge each other for overnight loans), sat between 0 and 0.25 percent. Interest rates had nowhere to go but up, and when interest rates rise, banks and other dividend investments, including utilities, may feel the pinch.

Which companies qualify

The financial services sector (financials, for short), includes commercial banks, savings & loans, mortgage companies, investment banks, stockbrokers, asset managers, mutual fund companies, credit services, and insurance companies. As demonstrated during the crash of 2008, these financials can generally be divided into two groups:

- ✔ **Risky investments:** Investment banks, brokerages, asset managers, and mutual fund companies are very volatile, following the fortunes of Wall Street.

- ✔ **Conservative propositions:** Commercial banks, regional banks, and insurance companies are more stable, and when you're talking dividend investing, you're looking for stability.

Evaluating banks' income-generating capabilities

Banks are pretty simple operations. They take money from depositors and then lend it to borrowers. Much more than manufacturers or service providers, a bank's profitability is intimately linked to its balance sheet. Its assets consist of all of its loans: personal, commercial, and mortgages, and whatever securities it holds and collects interest from. The liabilities are customer deposits on which it pays interest. This situation opens banks up to unique risks not seen in other industries.

Banks want the rate they receive on loans to be much higher than the rate they pay savings accounts. If the bank charges 6 percent for loans and pays only 1 percent on interest, the net interest spread is 5 percentage points. If the net interest spread turns negative, the bank is paying more out to depositors than it's collecting in interest on loans — a recipe for losing money.

Profits come from the difference in the actual interest revenue the bank's assets generate and the interest expense it pays out on its liabilities. This profit is called the *net interest income.* The net interest income must be large enough to cover all the bank's operating costs in order to post a profit and pay dividends. See "Calculating the net interest income" later in this chapter to determine this number for a particular bank.

Assessing banks

When banks go belly up, investors can lose everything, so if you're considering investing in a certain bank, take a close look at its financials. Some of the financials are the same as those I explain for other sectors in Chapter 9, but with banks, you have to look at a few additional numbers. The following sections highlight the most important numbers to consider.

The main factor contributing to a bank losing money is bad loans, so check the quality of the bank's assets (its loans) carefully.

Eliminating the riskiest candidates

When evaluating banks, eliminate the riskiest of the bunch by looking for the following red flags:

- **Bailout recipients:** Cut banks that received bailout money from the U.S. government right off your list. Let the government take the risk.

- **Dividend cuts:** Unless the bank has increased its dividend after making a cut, avoid it. Over 2009, many companies that cut or eliminated their dividends continued to perform poorly, and that's not just a recent phenomenon. According to Ned Davis Research, stocks that cut or eliminated their dividends have significantly underperformed the S&P 500 over the past 40 years.

Dividends are sacred cows. Management typically wants to do everything it can to avoid a cut. But after it's gone down that road, there's nothing to stop it from cutting the dividend again. In addition, a cut dividend means the managers have proven themselves to be fiscally irresponsible, poor managers of risk, and not looking out for shareholders. Make sure the management that brought the bank low has been dismissed before you put money into it.

If you choose to invest in banks, stay on top of the foreclosure statistics for both commercial and residential real-estate. Foreclosure is a very volatile area of the economy these days.

Focusing on banks that make the cut

Avoiding all financials may negatively affect your portfolio. If large banks no longer pay a dividend, take a look at regional banks that have been paying dividends for years and look like value plays. Canada's five major banks also provide a good way to get financial exposure. Toronto-Dominion Bank (TD), Bank of Montreal (BMO), Royal Bank of Canada (RY), Canadian Imperial Bank of Commerce (CIBC), and Bank of Nova Scotia (BNS) appear to have escaped the crisis no worse for wear. They continue to pay decent yields and haven't experienced any cuts.

The insurance sector is another financial group that has a history of dependable dividend growth and still pays decent yields. And although AIG remains the insurance industry's poster child for bad behavior, many insurance companies did what they were supposed to do. They managed their risk and cash flow very well and came out strong. The Chubb (CB) and Aflac (AFL) are two companies paying decent yields.

Checking the return on equity

Return on equity (ROE) determines the shareholders' rate of return. (For a full explanation, including the formula, see Chapter 8.) Scratch any bank off your list that doesn't have an ROE of at least 15 percent.

Calculating the net interest income

Net interest income is the difference between what the bank earns collecting interest from borrowers minus what it pays out in interest to depositors. Check the bank's most recent balance sheet to see the interest earned off of its total assets (loans, leases, and other debt instruments) and the interest paid on its total liabilities (deposit). Then do the math:

$$\text{Net Interest Income} = \text{Interest Earned on Assets} - \text{Interest Paid on Liabilities}$$

The net interest income must be sufficient to cover all the bank's operating costs *and* pay dividends. If the bank can't cover the dividend payments, scratch it off your list.

Assessing the equity/asset ratio

The equity/asset ratio tells you the bank's cushion in the event that its assets begin to lose value. Obtain the two values you need (shareholder equity and asset values) from the bank's most recent balance sheet. Then, do the math:

Equity/Asset Ratio = Shareholders' Equity ÷ Total Assets

The higher the number here, the better. Conservative lenders can get away with a ratio of 5 percent. However, if you're looking at smaller banks or riskier lenders, the ratio should be more than 8 percent.

Evaluating the charge-off ratio

Charge-offs are bad loans — the ones the bank expects to lose money on. This number is typically hidden somewhere in a quarterly report's footnotes. You want to see a low charge-off ratio — less than 1 percent. You also want to look for consistent results to make sure the year you're looking at isn't a fluke either way — positive or negative.

Investigating nonperforming assets

Isn't that a great name? *Nonperforming assets* makes it sound like they're on a break. And, well, they are. They're loans the borrowers have stopped making payments on. Nonperforming assets become bad loans when they go into default. This statistic is also typically found in the footnotes of the earnings reports, right near the charge-off ratio. Growth in this category is a bad sign.

Looking into the efficiency ratio

The efficiency ratio measures how well the bank keeps down its operating costs, also known as overhead. Rising costs cut into profits. To measure a bank's efficiency, perform any one (or all) of the following four formulas; you can find the values you need on the company's annual report or 10-K:

Noninterest Expenses ÷ (Total Revenue – Interest Expense)

Noninterest Expenses ÷ Net Interest Income before Provision for Loan Losses

Noninterest Expenses ÷ Revenue

Operating Expenses ÷ (Fee Income + Tax Equivalent Net Interest Income)

Look for banks with an efficiency ratio of 50 percent or lower — the lower, the better. As operating costs eat up more of the profit, the efficiency ratio rises.

Checking out the payout ratio

The *payout ratio* is the percentage of profits being used to pay the dividend. For a full explanation, complete with the necessary formula, check out Chapter 8.

Bank payout ratios typically reside around 50 percent. If the ratio rises, is it because the bank has no opportunities to invest the money and grow the company, or is it having a bad year? Neither of these is a good sign, but don't base your decision solely on payout ratio; do more investigating.

Chapter 6

Dividend Investment Vehicles

· ·

In This Chapter

▶ Exploring the pros and cons of investing through DRIPs

▶ Getting up to speed on mutual funds

▶ Introducing exchange-traded funds (ETFs)

▶ Scoping out the advantages and disadvantages of global dividend investing

· ·

*B*uying shares in a company is sort of like buying cereal. You can purchase one big box of a particular cereal or an assortment. In the world of investing, you have even more options: dividend reinvestment plans (DRIPs), direct purchase programs (DPPs), mutual funds, exchange-traded funds (ETFs), and foreign dividend funds, to name the most popular of the lot.

Don't let the acronyms and investor jargon scare you off. In this chapter, I explain each of these options in turn, and in plain English; discuss their pros and cons; and show you how to implement them in your dividend investment strategy.

The Nature of DRIPs and DIPs

A *dividend reinvestment plan* (DRIP) is a type of *direct investment plan* (DIP). Instead of buying shares on the stock market, you purchase shares directly from the company on a regular basis. Dividends automatically go toward purchasing additional shares, and in many plans you can buy additional shares outside of the dividend-funded purchase, either as a one-time purchase or on a regular basis.

These plans go under a variety of names, but they all refer to essentially the same thing:

- ✔ Direct purchase plans (DPPs)
- ✔ Direct stock purchase plans (DSPs)
- ✔ Direct enrollment stock purchase plans (DESPs)
- ✔ No-load stock purchase plans

If you need some of that dividend money, many plans offer the option of reinvesting only a portion of your dividends and letting you take the remaining dividends as cash.

When you invest through a DRIP, you and the company make a long-term commitment to one another. Every dollar you invest and reinvest is a vote of confidence in the company and its management. To earn your vote, the company is motivated to remain profitable and grow, and with money from you and other investors, it has the capital to do just that.

Don't let the fact that a company has a DRIP or a DIP be the reason you invest in it. Research the company's fundamentals first. Only after identifying companies you want to invest in should you concern yourself with whether the companies offer DRIPs or DIPs.

The difference between DRIPs and DSPs

DRIPs and DSPs are kissin' cousins, not identical twins. Both DRIPs and DSPs allow you to reinvest dividends and purchase additional shares of stock. The big difference between the two is that DRIPs still mandate buying your first share through a stockbroker and then enrolling in the plan by submitting an application and the stock certificate. DSPs allow you to enroll in the plan when you buy your first share of stock.

At first glance, DSPs seem like the better deal: hassle-free, without the restrictions imposed on DRIPs. However, DRIPs comprise most of the low- or no-fee plans, whereas many DSPs carry significant fees and even commissions. For more about costs, head to "Looking out for fees" later in this chapter.

How plans are administered

Companies vary in how they administer their direct investment plans. Some administer the plans themselves, whereas others work through a transfer agent.

- ✔ **Company:** Some companies have the internal resources to manage their own DRIPs. You may not need to enroll in a DRIP to buy company stock, but you do have to enroll to have your dividends reinvested.

- ✔ **Transfer agent:** A *transfer agent* is a financial institution that specializes in recordkeeping for entities with many small investors, such as publicly traded companies and mutual funds. Transfer agents record every transaction in the account — deposits and withdrawals. They also produce and send investor mailings, and issue stock certificates.

The potential advantages of DRIPs

With DRIPs, the advantages tend to carry more weight than the disadvantages for long-term dividend investors, but they make little sense for investors who have a high turnover in their portfolios or need to keep their assets more liquid. For dividend stock investors who are looking to build wealth over the long haul, few (if any) investment programs can compete with the many advantages DRIPs offer.

Getting started on a shoestring budget

DRIPs are very similar to mutual funds in that they're good for investors starting out with very little capital. With a minimal investment, you can purchase stock in small quantities with low or no fees.

The one big difference is that mutual funds provide you with a portfolio that's diversified to some degree. With DRIP purchases, you own the stock of just one company. Sure, you can diversify your portfolio by enrolling in a number of DRIPs, but it's more costly and complicated than buying mutual fund shares.

One major benefit of DRIPs over mutual funds is that with DRIPs, you don't get stuck paying another investor's tax bill. As I explain in Chapter 11, you have to be careful about your timing when you're buying mutual funds so that you don't end up paying taxes on profits that someone else collected.

Investing at your own pace

Although all DRIPs require a minimum investment to join the plan, you generally have the luxury of investing at your own pace. On top of reinvesting dividends on a regular schedule, these plans offer you the ability to buy more shares through the plan, often with no commissions. This enables you to make additional investments — regularly or only when you have some extra money to invest.

Here's what you can expect:

- For most plans, the minimum investment can be as little as a single share.

- Some DPPs have a minimum investment requirement between $250 and $1,000.

- You may be able to buy additional shares commission-free through optional cash purchase plans (OCPs). Many of these plans allow you to invest as little as $10 at a time, although most set the minimum between $25 and $50 with a maximum close to $10,000. Check the fee structure before investing.

Saving on broker commissions

DRIPs eliminate the middleman (the broker who charges a commission to process every transaction) because you purchase stock directly from the company that issues it, saving you a ton of money in transaction costs. Compared to a mutual fund, you avoid the load charged every time you make an investment and the hefty management fees deducted from the fund's assets.

Taking the emotion out of stock investing

Investing can get emotional. When you buy a DRIP and commit to investing on a regular schedule, the market's movements have little effect on how you invest. In good times and bad, you calmly and coolly acquire shares, building wealth slowly and more surely.

Compounding growth one drip at a time

Investing in a DRIP means you don't receive a dividend check tempting you to cash it out and fly to Aruba or use it to pay bills. Every penny in dividends is automatically reinvested for you to purchase additional shares of the company. These additional shares produce dividends, too. By allowing the dividends to be reinvested, you tap into the power of compounding growth without ever having to think about it.

Purchasing fractional ownership

When you purchase stock through a broker, you can't buy a half or a third of a share. With most DRIPs, as with mutual funds, you can. Suppose you earn $100 in dividends, and shares cost $35. Instead of buying only two shares for $70 and having the extra $30 sitting on the sidelines, you can buy 2.86 shares and put all that money to work for you immediately.

When the next dividend distribution rolls around, you get a fraction of the dividend based on the fractional share you own. If the quarterly dividend per share is 50 cents, you earn $1.43 for those 2.86 shares you purchased: 50 cents each for the two whole shares and then 43 cents for the 0.86 shares. ($.50 × 0.86 = $.43).

Dollar cost averaging without lifting a finger

DRIPs are a perfect way to implement a *dollar cost averaging* strategy — investing a fixed (or in the case of DRIPs, a semi-fixed) amount of money regularly over time. You don't have to lift a finger because the plan automatically reinvests your dividends for you, purchasing shares on a regular basis regardless of current market conditions or share price.

The downside of DRIPs

After ticking off the many benefits of DRIPs, you may be tempted to dump your broker and deal direct. Not so fast. As with most things in the world of investing, DRIPs have a flip side — some potential negatives to counterbalance all those positives. Before breaking up with your broker, consider the potential drawbacks highlighted in the following sections.

Buying on the company's schedule

When you reinvest dividends, you get a bargain because you buy the new shares right after prices drop due to the dividend payout, giving you more stock for your dividend dollars. However, you may lose out when the time comes to make other stock purchases. You have no control over the price you pay for optional cash purchases, which occur on the company's schedule, not yours. A company may choose to sell OCP shares once a week, once a month, or even once a quarter. If the stock happens to hit an all-time high that day, well, that's your price.

Losing liquidity

When you buy and sell stocks through a broker, you can cash out at any time. Just pick up the phone and tell your broker to sell, or log in to your online brokerage account and issue a sell order. The trade occurs within minutes, and in a matter of hours or days you have the money. When buying and selling shares directly through a company, you relinquish that liquidity. You must contact the company or the plan's transfer agent; obtain, complete, and submit the necessary forms for closing out the DRIP; and then wait for your request to be approved. This process can take a few weeks and may be an available option only once a quarter. You may also incur some fees for closing the account.

Looking out for fees

Although DRIPs are cheap and commission-free, only about half the DRIPs are totally fee-free. As money gets tight, more companies try to quietly slip in fees. As for DSPs, most charge fees, some on every transaction. To protect yourself, read the prospectus to find out what all the fees in the plan are and whether any terms seem unreasonable. Some companies charge $5 for an investment of as little as $25.

Check the plan's prospectus (included with the application packet) for any of the following fees:

- ✔ Setup fees to establish the account may run as high as $25.

- ✔ Termination fees to close the account may run anywhere from $5 to $25.

- ✔ Commissions (yes, commissions) in DSPs can be a flat fee between $2 and $25, a percentage of the amount invested, or a per-share charge of anywhere from a penny to 15 cents a share.

A company may nickel and dime you to the point at which you're kicking yourself for not paying your broker $10 for the transaction.

Don't let fees automatically scare you off. If you really like the stock, a direct purchase may still be the more cost-effective way to buy shares.

Paying taxes in a DRIP

Even though you don't receive a check for all those reinvested dividends, the IRS considers them taxable income. Plan for the following (and check out Chapter 11 for more on potential tax issues and qualified dividends):

- ✔ Dividends earned from new shares purchased through a reinvestment plan the previous quarter are taxed as *qualified* dividends — as in qualified for a lower tax rate.

- ✔ Dividends from new shares purchased through an OCP must meet the holding period requirements to qualify for the lower tax rate.

Keeping detailed records

For all their benefits, DRIPs provide you with one big fat pain in the neck: recordkeeping. Though you may get a neat printout from the company's transfer agent showing all your trades and tallying which dividends and capital gains qualify for reduced tax rates, you may not. Either way, you alone are responsible for keeping track of each purchase, including the date, number of shares purchased, and price paid, so you know exactly how much you owe in taxes when you sell your shares.

Calculating the cost basis of shares acquired through DRIPs

One of the main challenges of managing DRIPs is calculating the *cost basis* (how much money you pay for your shares) of your investment for tax purposes. As you make additional investments in a company and reinvest your dividends, you pay a different price for each batch of shares you purchase, so your cost basis can vary among the shares you own and changes with each transaction. Unfortunately, you can't simply use an average cost basis when calculating the taxes you owe on shares you sell, so you need to keep track of each purchase to know the cost basis of each share.

For tax purposes, keep track of the following information:

✔ Total amount of money spent and total number of shares acquired with each purchase.

✔ Dividends paid, even if they're reinvested, because dividends are taxed separately.

✔ Any discounts the company provides when you purchase shares. This discount qualifies as an additional dividend.

✔ Total amount of money and total number of shares acquired with each dividend reinvestment.

✔ Any commissions you paid to purchase shares, which can help offset taxes due on dividend payments.

✔ Total amount of money received when selling shares and the total number of shares sold.

When selling shares, follow a *first in, first out* (FIFO) strategy in determining your capital gains. In other words, the first shares you purchase are the first shares you sell. This method increases your holding period so that you're more likely to qualify for the lower long-term capital gains tax rate. (Flip to Chapter 11 for details on taxation concerns.)

Diversifying Your Dividends through Mutual Funds

Mutual funds are investment companies that pool money from many investors to buy securities and create a portfolio more diverse than most investors would be able to assemble on their own. Each investor shares in the fund's profit or loss according to the number of shares they own. The fund brings in more investing money by selling shares of the portfolio to the public. As an open-end investment company, the mutual fund can sell as many shares as people want to buy, using the money to purchase additional assets.

The advantages of mutual funds

Owning shares of a mutual fund is a trade-off. Mutual funds provide investors with an easier way to build and manage a diversified portfolio, but investors relinquish control over which stocks the portfolio holds. That's the biggie.

Mutual funds offer a host of benefits that essentially boil down to simplicity and diversity. Mutual funds

- ✔ Are easy to buy and sell

- ✔ Offer a diversified portfolio with a minimal investment

- ✔ Are run by a professional portfolio manager who does all the research and decides which securities to buy

- ✔ Work well with the dollar cost averaging strategy (discussed later in this chapter)

- ✔ Require little work from investors

- ✔ Are regulated by the SEC

- ✔ Reinvest dividends

- ✔ Keep track of all the bookkeeping involved

- ✔ Allow for redemptions over the phone

- ✔ Permit the purchase of fractional shares

A *fractional share* is a part of a share. If you plan to invest $100 a month to buy shares of a favorite stock selling for $75 a share, you can only buy one share because stocks sell in whole units. You then have $25 sitting around until you come up with another $50. However, if you invest with a mutual fund, the fund invests the entire $100. If one share of the mutual fund sells for $75, the fund sells you 1⅓ shares of the fund.

Mutual funds' cons

Many of the disadvantages of mutual funds are simply the flip side of the advantages — you willingly relinquish control over which equities are included in the portfolio because you don't have the time, energy, or inclination to do the research yourself. However, before you invest in a mutual fund, be aware of the following drawbacks:

- ✔ Mutual funds charge management fees.

- ✔ All taxes are passed on to and paid by the shareholders.

✔ Some charge big commissions.

✔ Shares don't trade like stocks — they have only one price during the day.

✔ The actions of other investors in the fund affect the amount of capital gains taxes you pay.

✔ Mutual funds may incur other costs, such as transaction fees for the stocks it buys and sells.

Diversification

Suppose you have only $2,000 to invest. One option is to purchase 80 shares of a small pharmaceutical company at 25 bucks a pop. Unfortunately, this option leaves you with a very concentrated portfolio. If the company's blockbuster drug fails to earn FDA approval, you stand to lose a good chunk of your investment. Another option is to purchase 10 shares of 20 different companies for $10 apiece. This strategy gives you some diversity, but the transaction fees take a bite out of that $2,000. A third option is to purchase $2,000 worth of shares in a mutual fund with 500 different stocks in its portfolio. Option three gives you a far more diversified portfolio than the other two options, without the added cost of commissions (though you likely pay management fees). Even with a management fee, this route is still usually less than paying commissions.

Dollar cost averaging

Dollar cost averaging is a method of systematically investing in anything over a long time period to achieve a reasonable average price for the asset. Mutual funds are great vehicles for following a dollar cost averaging strategy for a couple of reasons:

✔ You can buy a little at a time without having to pay a broker for every purchase.

✔ You can buy fractional shares. In a no-load fund (where you pay no commission), the ability to buy fractional shares means every single dollar you invest goes into the fund and goes to work immediately instead of sitting in cash waiting for enough to buy a full share.

How funds pay dividends

Funds are required to distribute any income in excess of their expenses. If the dividend yield is 1 percent of the fund's assets, and the expense ratio (operating expenses) is 1 percent of the fund's assets, the fund uses the dividend to pay the expenses, and investors receive no income. On the other hand, if the dividend yield is 3 percent of the fund's assets, the fund uses 1 percent to pay the expenses and then distributes the remaining 2 percent as dividends. If the mutual fund is focused on producing income, it will pay a dividend.

Mutual funds receive dividends much the same way as individual investors do. The companies whose shares the fund holds mail checks to the fund for the dividend amount. At the end of either every month or every fiscal quarter, the fund adds up all the dividends received from its holdings and divides by the total number of shares to determine the amount of dividends per fund share.

If the fund pays out too much "income," some of it can be classified as a return on capital, which falls under capital gains for tax purposes. See "Getting stuck paying taxes" later in this chapter for more about how returns on mutual fund investments are taxed.

A necessary evil: Paying a fund manager

When you invest in a mutual fund, you're hiring a professional — the individual running the fund — to manage your investments. Unfortunately, this person doesn't work for free. Managing a diversified portfolio that earns reasonable returns requires some expertise, time, and effort — all of which you pay for either in fees or commissions.

Some fund managers earn their keep, and many don't. All charge fees that can put a serious dent in the money you have available to invest, and they may perform no better than a standard S&P 500 Index fund that charges next to nothing. When investing in mutual funds, you really need to look at the costs to maximize the net return on your investment.

You can never guarantee the returns your fund will produce; however, you can always know what the fees will be. Your goal is to find a fund that produces the most consistent, and hopefully largest, return for the smallest amount of expenses. (Be aware that annual reports from mutual funds typically show the performance of the fund prior to deducting expenses and loads.)

Avoid funds with high expense ratios and loads. These costs can significantly reduce your capital gains.

Analyzing a fund's management style

Choosing a mutual fund is often a matter of choosing a management style, investment theme, or even a specific fund manager. All mutual funds follow an investing theme, such as buying the stocks of large U.S. companies or the bonds of emerging market economies. Some funds and their managers are very proactive in managing the portfolio: They may buy and sell shares daily to maximize the funds' returns. Others are more passive, building a solid portfolio and adjusting its holdings only occasionally, if at all.

In *actively managed funds,* the manager has the freedom to buy and sell whatever stock or bond she wants, whenever she wants, as long as she stays within the investing theme. Almost every mutual fund that follows a dividend-based or income-focused strategy is actively managed, but many don't charge a load (see the following section).

With a *passively managed fund,* the manager receives not just a theme but typically also an index to track, such as the S&P 500 Index or the Russell 2000 Index. He doesn't have the freedom to buy and sell whatever stocks he wants; he's locked into the index. Because the portfolio must perform in line with the index, he buys only the index components or a close approximation. Index funds are classic examples of passively managed mutual funds.

Accounting for expense ratios

Every fund is required to state its *expense ratio* or annual operating expenses. The expense ratio breaks down into three parts: management fees, 12b-1 costs, and other expenses.

✔ **Management fees:** Managers of active funds must hire research staffs to scope out new investments on a continual basis. They also need to keep on top of all market developments to buy and sell securities at the best time to maximize profits. On top of that, the managers need to manage all the other functions that a mutual fund performs, including accounting, record keeping, administration, and distribution, to name a few.

Management fees for passively managed funds are significantly lower than management fees for actively managed funds because managers of passive funds don't have the added expenses of research or stock selection.

✔ **12b-1 fees:** This special marketing fee (named after a section of the 1940 Act) pays for promotion and advertising of the fund. Some people think it's a hidden commission, but it basically goes to pay brokers to keep selling these funds. The fee is typically 0.25 percent, but can go as high as 1 percent.

✔ **Operating expenses:** This all-encompassing category covers all the other costs necessary to run the fund, paying for the fund's administrator, custodian, transfer agent, accountant, index provider, and distributor.

The average expense ratio for an actively managed fund is about 1.3 percent of the fund's total assets, and the management fees typically account for the lion's share of that figure. The nice thing about paying a percentage rather than a set fee is that the fund manager's interests are more aligned with yours. If your assets increase in value, she makes more money. If your assets decrease in value, she makes less money. Paying a management fee isn't necessarily a bad thing as long as the return you receive justifies the fees.

Paying for the privilege with loads

Because mutual funds don't trade on the stock exchange, brokers can't charge a typical commission, so they charge a special commission called a *load,* which is another cost on top of the expense ratio. There are three different kinds of loads: front-end load, back-end load, and no load.

✔ **Front-end load:** The front-end load is a percentage of your investment taken off the top and paid to the broker at the front end of the investment — the moment you buy shares. For instance, if you buy $100 worth of shares in a fund with a 5-percent load, you pay the broker $5 and invest $95 in the fund. You immediately invest less than you wanted to, which decreases your returns going forward. Typically, the shares that charge a front-end load are called *Class A shares.*

✔ **Back-end load:** In the back-end load, the broker takes his percentage when you sell your shares rather than when you buy them. If you sell $1,000 worth of fund shares, the fund with a 5-percent back-end load pays the broker $50 and leaves you with $950. Because the object is to have more money coming out of the fund than going in, the broker stands to make more with a back-load fund than with a front-load fund. However, the percentage of a back-end load gets smaller every year until it disappears five to ten years after the investment, so if you're in the fund for the very long term, you can avoid paying a back-end load when you sell. *Class B shares* typically charge a back-end load.

✔ **No load:** No-load funds charge no load when you buy or sell your shares. Because you research the fund and fill out the forms to purchase it, you essentially pay yourself the broker's load, which, of course, you invest into the fund. Invest $1,000, and all of that money goes toward the purchase of shares. When you sell, you keep all the money, except for any taxes you owe on your gains. To maximize your profits, I recommend you buy only no-load funds.

The load goes to the financial advisor or stockbroker who sells you the fund, not the actual mutual fund or its managers.

Many funds with loads also sell their funds through 401(k) retirement plans as *Class C shares.* Because a 401(k) plan is a closed system with limited choices, the fund companies don't charge investors a load to invest within the 401(k). However, they do typically charge a higher expense ratio.

Because mutual funds' annual reports often show performance without accounting for load and expense deductions, a no-load fund with a small expense ratio may actually provide a bigger return on your investment than a fund with a high load and expense ratio that performs better.

Investing in Dividend-Focused Mutual Funds

Mutual funds abound, and many of them focus more on capital appreciation than on dividends and income, so you have to be selective. In the following sections, I explain how to dig up information on mutual funds, identify dividend-focused funds, and understand how share prices are calculated. In addition, I reveal how mutual funds pay out dividends and detail some of the tax implications related to these payouts.

Spotting dividend-focused mutual funds

When shopping for dividend-focused mutual funds, don't let the names of the funds confuse you. Some mutual funds that advertise themselves as dividend funds hold plenty of growth stocks, and many mutual funds that do deal exclusively in dividend stocks don't even have the word *dividend* in their name. What's a dividend investor to do?

The first step is to screen for dividend funds. You can do so using online tools from Morningstar, Lipper, or Charles Schwab. For example, the Lipper Leaders website enables you to screen for Equity Income Funds.

Another strategy is to look for funds that have any of the following words in their names: *total return, income,* or *value.* Some income funds or blend funds can also hold bonds, generating income from both stocks and bonds, but searching for income or value funds should screen out most of the funds that have nothing to do with dividends.

When researching funds, carefully examine their holdings to determine what portion of the portfolio is comprised of companies that pay dividends. In the fund's prospectus, read its investment objective to determine what kind of strategy you're getting into. Look for mutual funds that have a yield greater than the yield on the S&P 500 Index. Any funds that fall short of this benchmark don't really qualify as dividend funds. Even among funds that focus on dividends, you can find significant differences in strategy and goals.

As with dividend stocks, you want to look for funds that raise their dividend distribution, because they invest in companies that consistently increase their payouts. A fund that has a rising dividend is making good investment choices from the payout perspective. And just like dividend stocks, you want the dividend fund to have regular payouts and less volatility than growth funds.

Understanding a fund's share price

Shares of mutual funds are sold and priced differently than shares of stock. Shares of stock trade on the stock exchange between investors. The market drives the price, which can rise or fall throughout the day according to investor demand. On the other hand, you buy mutual fund shares directly from the fund.

To determine the mutual fund's share price the fund company first calculates its *net asset value* (NAV). When the market closes, the fund obtains the end-of-day price for every equity held in the portfolio and multiplies each separate value by the number of shares the fund holds of that particular equity to determine its value. It then adds up the values of all equities in the portfolio and subtracts any liabilities to determine the NAV:

NAV = Total Value of All Equities – Liabilities

If the fund has $30 million in stocks and liabilities of $3 million, the NAV would be $27 million:

$30 million – $3 million = $27 million

To calculate the share price or NAV per share, the fund divides the NAV by the total number of shares sold to investors. Continuing from the previous example, if the fund sold 900,000 shares to investors, the NAV per share would be $30:

$27 million ÷ 900,000 shares = $30/share

Although you must place an order to buy or sell shares of a mutual fund when the stock market is open, you don't know what price you will pay. That's because the fund needs the closing price of every equity before it can calculate the NAV, and it can't get that until after the market's 4:00 p.m. close.

Reinvesting mutual fund dividends

When you first invest in a mutual fund that holds shares in companies that pay dividends, you need to specify what you want to do with the dividends. Typically, you have three choices:

- ✔ **Leave the cash in an account:** Your money just sits there until you tell the fund manager what to do with it.

- ✔ **Get a check:** Taking your cash when the fund announces its dividend payout enables you to do whatever you want with the dividend.

- ✔ **Reinvest the dividend:** Mutual funds make reinvesting the dividend very easy. They simply use the dividends to buy more fund shares and send you a statement to show you how much you bought. For most funds, reinvesting the dividend is the default option and the best choice for long-term growth and income.

  An added benefit of reinvesting is that the share prices fall after their ex-dividend dates (see Chapter 2 for more on the significance of this date). This drop lowers the fund's NAV, and because the fund doesn't receive the dividends until after the ex-dividend date, it reinvests them for you at the lower NAV.

Getting stuck paying taxes

Dividends from mutual funds are taxed just like dividends from stocks; those that don't qualify for the 15-percent tax rate are taxed at your ordinary income tax rate. However, mutual funds don't pay taxes. Mutual fund investors do.

Mutual funds are called *pass-through vehicles* because the tax liability passes through the fund to the shareholder. In addition, because actively managed mutual funds buy and sell shares on a regular basis, they earn significant capital gains. At the end of the year, the fund sends you a tax form telling you how much of these capital gains are short-term gains and how much are long-term gains. *Short-term gains* (on securities held for less than a year) are taxed at your ordinary tax rate, and long-term gains are taxed at a lower rate. For a detailed explanation of which dividends qualify for lower tax rates, head to Chapter 11.

Good funds manage their payouts so that most dividends qualify for the lower tax rate. Part of your research should look at how much of the dividends that the fund pays out qualify for the lower tax rate and what percentage of dividends don't. Obviously, you want a fund that pays out a very high percentage of dividends that qualify for the lower tax rate.

Spotting a good pick: A checklist

Typically, if you buy an actively managed fund, you're paying the fund manager to produce returns that beat his market benchmark. For large U.S. equity funds, that benchmark is the S&P 500; for small U.S. equity funds, it's the Russell 2000. For a dividend fund, you're obviously more concerned with making income, so you give up some potential for capital appreciation from non-dividend paying stocks in exchange for immediate income and less volatility.

In other words, as a dividend investor, you shouldn't expect the fund's return from capital appreciation to beat an index that holds growth stocks. However, you do want to see less volatility in the NAV and that the fund's total return with dividend income comes close to the index.

Now that you know now to evaluate mutual funds, look for funds that meet or exceed the following criteria:

- ✔ **No load:** The amount of money you lose to loads can significantly decrease your portfolio and its potential for capital gains. (Flip to the earlier section "Paying for the privilege with loads" for more on these expenses.)

- ✔ **Expense ratio below 2 percent:** Expense ratio fees also eat into your capital appreciation, as I discuss in the earlier section "Accounting for expense ratios." Make sure the dividend yield exceeds the expense ratio so that your income covers your costs and then some. That way you at least capture all the fund's capital appreciation, even though you're spending some of your dividends. The higher the fees, the less likely the returns from the fund will actually beat the market. I would never buy a fund that charges an expense ratio higher than 2 percent.

✓ **Fund's 12-month yield exceeds the 12-month yield of the benchmark index:** If the fund's 12-month yield doesn't beat the index, you're better off buying the index fund. From December 1936 through March 2009, the average yield for the S&P 500 Index was 3.814 percent. At the end of 2009, the S&P 500's 12-month dividend yield was 2.01 percent versus the 3.14 percent yield for December 2008. The yield is based on the cash dividends paid over the prior four quarters and the closing quarterly price.

✓ **Minimum returns:** Remember that share prices fluctuate, so dividend investors are willing to give up big gains in capital appreciation in return for steady dividend payouts higher than the benchmark index's yield. Don't be afraid to look at funds with a total return that is 1 or 2 percentage points lower than the index.

✓ **Established:** Don't buy new funds. You want a fund with a track record — the longer the better. You want to be able to see how the fund performs in a variety of market conditions. Be wary of anything with less than a three-year record. If you know an experienced manager who is starting her own fund, you may invest a little bit, but consider this investment very risky until she builds a record.

✓ **Five-year-plus history of consistently increasing dividend payments:** After all the other criteria, this one really boils it all down. Plenty of no-load funds have decent yields, but as with dividend stocks, you want your dividends to grow. A five-year record shows that the manager knows how to consistently pick stocks that have growing dividends.

The Best of Both Worlds: Exchange-Traded Funds

The easiest way to think about ETFs is as mutual *funds* that *trade* on an *exchange* like stocks — hence, the name. Although the ETF determines its true NAV the same way every evening, during the trading day ETFs can move away from the NAV. ETFs trade like stocks based on the demand for shares, so their prices fluctuate throughout the 9:30-a.m.-to-4-p.m. session.

Behind the scenes with ETFs

A lot of the ETF's benefits come from the unique way the fund acquires the basket of securities it holds in its portfolio. Unlike mutual fund investors, ETF investors don't buy or sell their shares directly with the fund, but rather with other investors on the stock exchange. To get to the stock exchange, ETF shares go through a *creation process* with a select, small group of broker-dealers or specialists known as the *authorized participants,* or *APs.* That's because ETFs only sell shares in lots of 50,000 called *creation units.*

Basically, the AP and the ETF make a cashless trade. In order for the AP to get ETF shares, it must gather together a basket of securities that match the index the ETF tracks. To do this, the AP either buys the shares on the stock market or pulls them from its massive inventory of securities. For example, if the ETF tracks the S&P 500, the AP assembles a basket of 50,000 shares of each of the 500 companies in the S&P 500, in the proper weighting.

Then instead of paying cash, the AP exchanges its basket of securities for the ETF's creation unit. This even trade of stocks for ETF shares is called an *in-kind trade* and bypasses stockbrokers, avoiding commissions. Even more important, the cashless in-kind trade creates no taxable events, so the ETF almost never incurs capital gains. Thus, ETF investors rarely pay the capital gains taxes inflicted on mutual fund investors. For more on capital gains, see "Achieving greater tax efficiency" later in the chapter.

After the AP makes the in-kind trade, it takes the 50,000 newly minted ETF shares and sells them on the secondary market to investors large and small. If demand for ETF shares is great enough, the AP can form additional baskets of stock to trade for ETF creation units so that it has more ETF shares to sell. If demand drops, the AP can redeem a basket of ETF shares for a basket consisting of the original 50,000 shares.

ETFs come in two varieties: *open-end investment companies* (funds) or *unit investment trusts* (UITs). The main difference between them is that open-end funds have fund managers and UITs don't. However, neither type has restrictions on how many shares it can sell; ETFs can sell as many shares as needed to fill investor demand. And when investors want to sell, they redeem the shares back to the ETF, taking the shares out of circulation.

Advantages of ETFs

Although ETFs differ from mutual funds, they offer many of the same advantages, including the following:

- ✔ You can own part of a diversified portfolio with the minimal investment of just one share — no large, upfront investment required.
- ✔ ETFs are easy to buy and sell.
- ✔ Most ETFs are run by professional managers.
- ✔ Your workload as an investor is minimal.
- ✔ ETFs are regulated by the SEC.
- ✔ ETFs are good for asset allocation and focusing investment dollars on a particular industry, asset class, or segment of the market.

Unlike mutual funds, ETFs don't keep track of all the bookkeeping involved. Instead, your brokerage firm takes care of this service. Also, ETFs don't allow redemptions over the phone.

In addition, ETFs offer solutions to some of the disadvantages of owning mutual funds. Compared to mutual funds, ETFs offer

- ✔ Greater flexibility
- ✔ Lower fees
- ✔ Increased tax efficiency
- ✔ Greater transparency
- ✔ The ability to invest in a variety of asset classes, such as commodities and currencies. (In this chapter, I deal exclusively with equity — that is, stock — ETFs.)

I discuss these advantages in more detail in "Some unique ETF advantages" later in the chapter.

A few drawbacks of ETFs

ETFs offer several advantages over mutual funds, but they also have a few drawbacks that mutual funds don't:

- You can't buy fractional shares of an ETF.
- You must buy shares through a stockbroker and pay a commission.
- ETFs may not be cost effective for a dollar-cost averaging strategy in a taxable account.

Some unique ETF advantages

In "Advantages of ETFs" earlier in this chapter, I touch on some ways ETFs go above and beyond mutual funds in the benefits department. Because a short list just can't do all those extra advantages justice, I break them down here so you can get an idea of exactly what ETFs have to offer you.

Gaining flexibility

Without a doubt, the biggest improvement the ETF holds over the mutual fund is its ability to trade on the stock exchange. With a mutual fund, you issue a buy or sell order during the stock market's trading session, but your order won't be filled until market close. If the market happens to crash after you initiate a sale, you may end up selling at the lowest price of the day. If the market rallies after you decide to buy, you probably end up paying the highest price of the day. However, you can buy and sell ETFs just like shares of stock anytime during the day.

Time flexibility isn't the only aspect giving ETFs the win here; you also have more trading options. The ETF investor can use all the trading tools available to the dividend-stock investor. An ETF investor can

- Trade with market orders
- Place limit orders
- Place stop loss orders

✔ Sell ETF shares short

✔ Borrow against ETF shares

✔ Purchase ETF shares on margin

You can't use any of these trading orders with a mutual fund.

Reducing your cost of ownership

Almost every equity ETF is an *index fund* — a passively managed fund. Because index funds have low management costs, ETFs typically charge an *expense ratio* (amount of annual operating expenses) lower than almost all actively-managed mutual funds. In addition, they usually charge less than comparable index-based mutual funds.

For the most part, the ETF holds what's in the index. It has a manager, but the manager doesn't have the freedom to buy and sell what he wants as many mutual fund managers do. He needs the fund's performance to closely match the return of the index the fund is tracking, and the easiest way to do so is to hold all the stocks in the index.

An ETF manager may decide to buy options or futures to approximate the index's return without holding every component if the index is huge or holds a lot of small and/or illiquid stocks. If a big fund kept buying these shares, it would influence the movement of the share prices.

Investigating the expense ratio

The three components of the mutual fund expense ratio are management fee, 12b-1 fee, and other expenses. The ETF pays a management fee, but it's smaller than comparable index funds and dramatically smaller than actively-managed funds. ETFs avoid many of the costs and fees that mutual funds incur such as recordkeeping costs, fund administrator compensation, and bid-ask spreads.

Examining transaction fees

In a battle over low transaction fees, ETFs win hands-down. Because they acquire shares through in-kind exchanges, they avoid having to pay broker commissions altogether. Mutual funds, on the other hand, pay broker fees whenever they buy securities in response to increasing demand for mutual fund shares or they buy or sell securities to adjust the portfolio.

Achieving greater tax efficiency

The ETF's tax efficiency comes from avoiding capital gains taxes inside the fund. Because ETFs don't buy or sell the securities held in their portfolios, they don't incur capital gains or need to pay capital gains taxes like mutual funds do. Capital gains taxes can add up quickly and come right out of your mutual fund returns. Because it's more tax efficient, the ETF leaves more money in your hands.

Of course, you still pay taxes when you buy and sell your ETF shares, but you maintain control of the tax strategy and timing. You can hold the shares a short period of time or for years. Just like shares in a company stock, you can take a capital gain or capital loss when it best suits your strategy. The mutual fund investor pays this same capital gains tax on the shares held in his fund account, in addition to the taxes from the capital gains on the stocks sold within the fund itself.

Increasing transparency

When dealing with fund managers, transparency is key. The ability to see what the ETF holds provides certain advantages, including the following:

- ✔ **You know exactly what you own and what you don't.**

- ✔ **You can avoid doubling up on stocks you already own through your funds.** By seeing what the fund holds, you can avoid owning what you don't like.

The *creation unit* (the 50,000 ETF shares traded to the AP) forces a transparency not required by the mutual fund. Because the AP (a broker or specialist called the *authorized participant*) needs to buy all the securities in the ETF to make an in-kind trade, the AP needs an updated list of stocks in the fund, so the ETF needs to publish this list daily. Mutual funds, on the other hand, are required to publish their portfolios only at the end of each quarter and have 60 days to release the information. Considering how much stock turnover can happen in an actively managed fund, the odds are pretty good that the end-of-quarter report is a poor reflection of the fund's current composition.

Comparing loads against commissions

You buy ETFs through a broker, which translates into paying commissions. When comparing mutual funds that charge a front-end or back-end *load* (special commission taken on either the purchase or sale of shares) to ETFs, paying broker commissions may cost you less. The percentage of your purchase you pay for a mutual fund load stays the same regardless of the dollar amount of your share purchase, but the percentage you pay in commissions decreases as the dollar amount of your ETF purchase rises. Investing $100 in a mutual fund with a front-end load of 5 percent costs you $5, while purchasing $100 worth of shares in an ETF may cost you a $10 commission (10 percent). Invest $10,000, however, and your 5 percent load rises to $500 while your ETF commission remains at $10, just 0.1 percent of your investment.

ETFs don't always win the load/commission battle with mutual funds, however. With a *no-load mutual fund,* you pay no commission. The advantage here clearly goes to the no-load mutual fund, but you can significantly reduce the commissions you pay by purchasing through a discount broker (for about $10 per trade) and buying in bulk: the bigger the purchase, the less of a percentage you pay in commissions.

Dividends from ETFs

Like mutual funds, ETFs maintain their tax-free status by distributing their dividends back to investors, usually on a quarterly basis. Typically, the fund sends dividend payments to the investor's brokerage account, but you may be able to reinvest the dividends.

When researching a dividend fund's holdings, determine how much of the fund actually holds dividend stocks. A fund that markets itself as a dividend fund isn't required to hold only dividend stocks. Check the fact sheet on the ETF's website to see which sector of the market the ETF's index tracks and what percentage of the portfolio holds dividend stocks. Typically, a dividend fund holds more than 80 percent in dividend stocks. Names other than "Dividend" that indicate the fund may be following a dividend strategy include "total return," "income," and "value."

Reinvesting dividends

As with any dividend investment, reinvesting your dividend payments is a key component of growing your assets. With ETFs, dividends can be reinvested at the fund level or the investor level, as I explain in the following sections.

Fund level

If the ETF is an open-end investment company, it can reinvest the dividends it receives from the stocks in its portfolio to buy more stocks. This strategy avoids the problem of *cash drag* (having a fund not fully invested in the market because the fund holds cash) on the portfolio and can help boost returns a little bit. Then when the fund needs cash to distribute dividends to the shareholders, it sells the shares, which may incur a capital gain.

ETFs structured as UITs don't have a manager or board of directors, so no one is available to reinvest the dividends. The cash sits in the ETF's account creating a cash drag until the quarterly dividend distribution. If the market rises, the stocks in the portfolio appreciate, but the cash doesn't generate interest, so it drags down the portfolio's total return.

The number of ETFs organized as UITs is pretty small, but this group includes some of the largest ETFs. In addition to the Spyder, others include the Dow Diamonds (DIA), which tracks the Dow Jones Industrial Average; the PowerShares QQQ (QQQQ), which follows the technology-heavy NASDAQ 100 Index; and the MidCap SPDR (MDY), which tracks the S&P MidCap 400 Index, a benchmark for midsized companies.

An open-end ETF that tracks the S&P 500 but doesn't have the cash drag of the Spyder is the iShares S&P 500 Index (IVV).

Shareholder level

Unlike a mutual fund, an ETF can't reinvest dividends for you. The ETF distributes the cash dividend to the investor's brokerage firm, typically at the end of each quarter. Some brokerage firms offer ETF investors the service of automatic dividend reinvestment for free, but some don't. If your broker doesn't offer this service, you have to pay another commission to reinvest your dividend by purchasing new shares.

Paying taxes on ETF dividends

Paying taxes on dividends is always a drag, but the ETF may be able to give you a break through its accounting practices. Qualifying dividends are eligible for a 15-percent tax rate, just like dividends you may receive from mutual funds and stocks. Most fund managers can manage the dividend payouts so that a larger portion qualifies for the lower tax rate.

 When researching ETFs, check the portion of dividend payouts that qualifies for the 15-percent tax rate. Look for ETFs that tend to pay out a very high percentage in qualified dividends.

Shaking WisdomTree's Family of Dividend Funds

Investors who want a pure dividend fund need to become acquainted with WisdomTree Investments. This New York firm has created a line of indexes comprised only of dividend stocks and launched a family of ETFs to track these indexes. These funds are the only ETFs comprised entirely of dividend stocks. The firm's benchmark is the WisdomTree Dividend Index, which holds every dividend-paying stock in the United States with a *market capitalization* (share price times total number of shares outstanding) greater than $100 million. The stocks also need to meet certain liquidity requirements. Every WisdomTree U.S. stock ETF is based on this index or an offshoot of it.

WisdomTree ETFs follow indexes that use dividend weighting. In dividend weighting, a company's index weighting is based on the actual dollar value of its annual dividend rather than its price as in market capitalization. To get the total dollar value of the dividend paid to shareholders, WisdomTree takes a company's dividend per share and multiplies it by the number of common shares outstanding. It compares this amount to the total dividend stream of all the companies in the index. The larger the dividend, the heavier the weighting. So a small company paying a big dividend can have a greater weighting than a large company paying a small dividend.

Going Global with Foreign Dividends

In the global economy, opportunities abound, but wherever you find opportunity, risk is right around the corner. In the following sections, I reveal the pros and cons of investing in global dividends so that you can make an educated decision about whether to invest globally and how much of your portfolio to allocate to foreign investments.

In terms of market capitalization, only 40 percent of the world's companies reside in the U.S. market. That means that by investing only in the U.S., you shut yourself off from more than half the investing opportunities worldwide. And if you look at an international index weighted according to where dividends are paid, 70 percent of those investments reside outside the U.S.

The advantages

In addition to keeping your portfolio from being tied to only one country's economy, investing in global dividend stocks offers several potential advantages in terms of expanding your opportunities and protecting your portfolio:

- **Expanding your investing universe.** Currently, a great deal of the economic growth in the world occurs outside the U.S., especially in emerging markets. With their educated populations looking for opportunities in a global market, Brazil, Russia, India, and China have seen astronomical growth in their economies. And they're just beginning their growth cycles.

- **Receiving higher yields.** The sad fact for dividend investors is that the U.S. is one of the lowest-yielding stock markets in the world. The 4-percent average yield in the developed world outside the U.S. is twice the yield on the S&P 500.

- **Collecting dividends from technology stocks.** Very few U.S. technology companies pay dividends, and those that do pay tiny yields. Yet many technology companies outside the U.S. pay dividends, and most with a sizeable yield. So if you follow a dividend strategy in the U.S.

and want a minimum yield of 3 percent, you have to buy American depositary receipts (see "Investing in American depositary receipts" later in this chapter) to avoid being severely underrepresented in the technology sector, which was the strongest sector in 2009.

✔ **Protecting your portfolio from weakness in the dollar.** When you invest in foreign companies that pay dividends, they pay profits in other currencies that may be stronger against the dollar. As a result, you may see more profit in terms of dollar amount when your profits are converted. If U.S. companies do business in foreign countries, you may see a similar benefit when the company's foreign profits are converted to dollars.

The disadvantages

Don't let talk of a struggling U.S. economy, a ballooning national debt, or a falling dollar lead you to immediately move all your money into foreign investments:

✔ **Taking on higher risk.** Investing in the U.S. may seem risky, but the risk levels in other countries may be nearly the same (such as in Western Europe and Japan) or even worse (like in emerging markets). The risks typically involve fluctuating currency, differences in (or lack of) regulation, and political shifts.

✔ **Paying a foreign withholding tax.** Foreign countries tax dividends too, so you often end up in a double-taxation scenario, having to pay foreign taxes along with U.S. taxes on dividends.

✔ **Dealing with variations in dividend payments.** In the U.S., companies typically pay dividends quarterly. When you invest in foreign countries, however, you can't count on companies following this same standard.

✔ **Accepting less transparency.** Many foreign markets have much less transparency than the U.S. market. This characteristic can mask conflicts of interest and sweetheart deals from the government. For many foreign companies, access to material information or even news stories can be difficult, making research a time-consuming chore.

✔ **Losing the international diversification advantage to globalization.** With financial institutions and multinational corporations crossing borders, markets are much more connected than ever before. The days of using one country as a safe haven while the rest of the world crumbles are quickly fading.

If you directly purchase a foreign stock outside the U.S., you're responsible for determining the correct foreign withholding tax so you can claim your tax credit. Failure to do so may result in a double-taxation scenario in which you lose your tax credit.

Examining Ways to Go Global

If you want to move your investment capital to foreign countries, and you live in the United States, you have three options: getting into American depository receipts, investing in global dividend-based mutual funds or ETFs, or buying shares on a foreign exchange. The following sections explore these options.

Investing in American depositary receipts

American depositary receipts, better known as ADRs, are by far the easiest way to buy and directly own foreign stocks in the United States. ADRs are dollar denominated and trade like equities on the U.S. stock market, but they aren't stocks. They're certificates issued by U.S. banks, which hold the underlying foreign shares in the local market and issue the certificates, or receipts, on the U.S. market to represent a specific number of the underlying security. Some ADRs represent two or more shares of the underlying stock.

ADRs offer several advantages over other methods of investing in foreign markets. ADRs

✔ Are *dollar denominated.* Shares trade in dollars, and dividends are paid in dollars.

✔ Trade on the U.S. market.

✔ Avoid currency issues.

✔ Reduce the huge administration and transaction costs involved with buying shares directly on a foreign exchange.

✔ Are regulated by the United States. Companies that trade as ADRs must file financial statements with the SEC.

✔ Pay dividends that qualify for lower tax rates, if you hold them the necessary holding period. For more about holding period requirements, check out Chapter 11.

Investing in ADRs comes with some potential disadvantages, including the following:

✔ The underwriter of an ADR charges a fee for its services. This cost is typically modest and transparent, but it comes directly out of your dividend.

✔ Usually only companies with a large capitalization become ADRs.

✔ Very few ADRs represent stocks in emerging economies.

✔ ADR performance can be difficult to predict due to currency exchange issues. You receive dividends in dollars, but they're paid in local currency and converted by the receipt issuer. A radical change in exchange rates can mean more or less money in dividends year over year. This swing makes predicting the actual dividend difficult even if it remains consistent in its home market.

Investing through a mutual fund or ETF

To buy foreign equities not available as ADRs, the best route is to buy an international mutual fund or ETF. Many mutual fund and ETF companies offer funds that track stocks abroad. You can buy a fund that tracks the whole world, including or excluding U.S. stocks. You can buy funds that invest in just one country or specific area of the market, such as only Europe or only Asia.

Mutual funds and ETFs take all the hassle, much of the cost, and some of the risk out of investing in foreign stocks by offering the following advantages:

- ✔ All the advantages of mutual funds and ETFs listed earlier in this chapter, such as building a diversified portfolio in which you can buy shares with a minimal investment
- ✔ Convenience
- ✔ Dollar denominated (see the preceding section for more on dollar denomination)
- ✔ Purchased in the U.S.
- ✔ Managed by professional U.S. asset managers with expertise in these markets who have researched and visited these foreign companies to gain firsthand insights and hard-to-access local information
- ✔ Financial institutions that can manage currency risk
- ✔ Management fees much less than the cost of buying many foreign stocks on your own

Buying directly on foreign exchanges

Many full-service brokers and even some discount brokers let you buy and sell equities directly on a foreign stock exchange. For stocks that don't trade as ADRs, buying directly offers one advantage and several potential disadvantages. The one sole advantage of direct trading on foreign exchanges is that you gain access to markets and stocks not represented by ADRs.

The potential disadvantages of direct trading on foreign exchanges abound. The main drawbacks are

- ✔ Higher transaction costs as the *bid-ask spread* widens. The *bid* is the highest price a buyer is willing to pay for a security, and the *ask* is the lowest price acceptable to the seller. The difference between them is the *spread*. The party that needs the trade done more quickly pays the spread.
- ✔ High administration costs because the broker charges for currency conversion.

✔ Greater currency risk. These stocks trade in the local currency.

✔ No protections provided by U.S. laws and regulation. The corporate governance structures of most foreign countries are much looser than the U.S.

✔ Less respect for shareholders' rights.

✔ Harder-to-find material information. These firms aren't required to file financial data with the SEC. Look to the company's website for information. Of course, many of these sites aren't in English.

✔ Smaller and riskier companies than those that trade as ADRs.

Part III

Selecting an Investment Approach

PAYER'S name, street address, city, state, ZIP code, and telephone no.		1a Total ordinary dividends $	OMB No. 1545-0110	Dividends and Distributions
		1b Qualified dividends $	**2009** Form **1099-DIV**	
		2a Total capital gain distr. $	2b Unrecap. Sec. 1250 gain $	**Copy A** For Internal Revenue Service Center File with Form 1096.
PAYER'S federal identification number	RECIPIENT'S identification number			
RECIPIENT'S name		2c Section 1202 gain $	2d Collectibles (28%) gain $	For Privacy Act and Paperwork Reduction Act Notice, see the **2009 General Instructions for Forms 1099, 1098, 3921, 3922, 5498, and W-2G.**
		3 Nondividend distributions $	4 Federal income tax withheld $	
Street address (including apt. no.)			5 Investment expenses $	
City, state, and ZIP code		6 Foreign tax paid $	7 Foreign country or U.S. possession	
Account number (see instructions)	2nd TIN not. ☐	8 Cash liquidation distributions $	9 Noncash liquidation distributions $	

Form **1099-DIV**   Cat. No. 14415N   Department of the Treasury - Internal Revenue Service

Get some tips for spotting dividend bargains www.
dummies.com/extras/investingindividends.

In this part . . .

- ✔ Figure out your own investment style so that you can set solid goals.

- ✔ Look deeply into risk and reward so that you can align your investments with your risk tolerance.

- ✔ Uncover three approaches to investing so you can march confidently ahead.

- ✔ Find out which facts and figures guide your choices and how to find them as you work to assess potential investments.

- ✔ Get down to action with all the details you need to choose a broker and start buying and selling.

- ✔ Brace yourself for the impact of taxes on your investments in the tricky world of dividends.

Chapter 7

Setting Goals and Making Plans

. . . .

In This Chapter

▶ Discovering your preferred investing style

▶ Defining your goals

. . . .

*B*efore you start plunking money into the stock market, realize that people don't invest in the stock market for the pure joy of owning stocks. Stocks are a means to an end, a way to parlay your savings into more money to finance what you want: a vacation home, a fancy car, your kids' or grandkids' education, a comfortable retirement, or whatever. To be a successful investor, you need to write down your financial goals and honestly analyze yourself. Does money burn a hole in your pocket? Are you a reckless spender? Are you afraid of taking risks, or are you more of a high roller?

Perhaps even more important is having a goal and a realistic time frame in mind — what do you want and how long do you have to acquire the money for it? Whether you need the money two years from now or 30 years down the road can have a strong influence over how you choose to invest your money.

A sincere and honest evaluation now can save you much time and agony later. This chapter helps you figure out what kind of investor you are, how aggressive you are (or aren't), what your goals are, and how much time you have to achieve your goals. With this information, you can begin to formulate and implement a practical investment plan for achieving your goals.

Your Personality Profile

Whenever you're about to engage in anything worth pursuing — career, marriage, child-rearing, community service — consider how your personality factors in. A fair portion of unhappy people are unhappy because they live life against the grain. They pursue a career they're not passionate about, marry someone who doesn't share their goals and values, or buy things they really don't find fulfilling.

The same is true of investing. If you tend to be a high roller, socking away your savings in a CD or money market account will probably bore you to tears. If you're more conservative, gambling big in the hopes for big returns will turn you into a nervous wreck. To choose an investment style that's right for you, take a moment to analyze your personality.

What's your style?

Wall Street considers an investor any person or business that buys an asset with the expectation of reaping a financial reward. However, I think this all-encompassing use of the term *investor* blurs important distinctions between the various market participants: savers, speculators, and investors.

The first step on the road to becoming a successful dividend investor consists of becoming a money saver. Whether you've been saving money for years or are just starting today, the fact is that you need to save more. After you become a saver, the question becomes whether you want to progress to speculating or investing to make your seed money grow. The following sections examine savers, speculators, and investors to help you figure out which approach matches your personality.

When I talk about short-term and long-term investments, I use the following time frames:

> ✔ **Short-term is two years or less.** Why two years? Because it rarely provides enough time to recoup losses. Look at the 2008 market crash. The S&P 500 hit its high in October 2007. A year and a half later the index lost half its value. Two years later, even though the market struck a bottom and began to bounce back, it remained significantly lower.

✔ *Intermediate* **is two to five years.** This period usually gives stocks enough time to recover — still no guarantee of a recovery, but chances are much better.

✔ *Long-term* **is five years or more.** When you can leave your money in the market for five years or more, you have a significant buffer for the ups and downs of the market.

Also, I consider a savings account to be long-term/short-term vehicle: Long-term, because you plan to hold it for many years; short-term because it provides liquid funds for immediate needs.

Saver

Every investor starts out as a saver. After all, you have to have some money before you can invest it. Some people move past this stage to become speculators or investors, but others remain savers throughout their lives.

What separates the saver from the speculator or investor is risk. The saver's main objective is capital preservation. After he's squirreled away some money from his paycheck, he wants to guarantee the cash will be there when he needs it. To achieve his goals, he tends to invest in safe vehicles — bank accounts, CDs, and money market accounts — because of their low risk, safety, and liquidity. The big down sides? Very little chance of capital appreciation and near certainty of inflation chipping away at that nest egg.

Speculator

Speculators attempt to capitalize on the market's short-term price movements — *volatility.* Capital preservation is a low- or no-priority item. The speculator jumps into the market and puts his principle at significant risk in the hopes of scoring a big return quickly. Unlike investors, speculators really have no interest in how long a company will be in business. Their sole focus is share price.

Volatility can best be described as the size and frequency of extreme price moves over short periods of time. *High volatility* means an asset's price can experience dramatic moves up or down, and *low volatility* describes moves of less than 5 percent.

Speculation can be day-trading a variety of stocks many times every single day or buying and holding a blue-chip stock for 12 months. If it sounds a lot like gambling, that's because it pretty much is. Speculating demands a high risk tolerance because you can easily lose money. Over the long-term, the stock market climbs higher. But over the short-term, asset markets can be extremely volatile. It's very similar to what happened with real estate investors who were flipping houses in 2006 and 2007, banking on rising real estate values and hoping for big returns. When the housing bubble burst, many were stuck with homes worth significantly less than what they had paid for them. Even worse, most of them didn't have the cash necessary to continue making payments. Speculating in the stock market can lead to similar results: If you have to sell in a down market, you almost certainly stand to lose money.

Investor

Investors are in the stock market for the long-haul, seeking both capital preservation and appreciation. As such, they're willing to take more risk than savers but approach their investments more carefully than speculators. Following are the three actions that define investors:

- ✔ They have long-term financial goals — several years rather than several months, days, or hours.
- ✔ They plan to hold long-term investments, holding an investment vehicle for at least five years.
- ✔ They do extensive research because they plan on holding their shares for five years or more and want to invest in fundamentally sound companies.

Because of the volatile nature of most financial vehicles, you can never be sure of selling them at a profit when you need the cash. If the stock market suffers a major downturn, even conservative investments can experience significant price drops. However, if you give your investments many years to grow, even if the market suffers a downturn, a portfolio with stable, dividend-paying stocks will be worth more than when you started.

How aggressive are you?

In Chapter 8, I explain how you can determine your risk tolerance. Some investors tend to be more aggressive than others — they want more, expect more, and are willing risk more to get it. Conservative investors, on the other hand, are either fairly satisfied with what they have (assuming their investments are growing at a steady rate and earning a reasonable return) or are fearful of losing what they've already acquired. In the following sections, I describe these two types of investors in greater detail and show how differences in aggressiveness can influence investment styles.

Conservative

The word *conservative* has nothing to do with politics when used in an investment context. Political conservatives can be very aggressive investors, and liberals can be very conservative in managing their money. In the world of investing, *conservative* means careful. Conservative investors tend to play it safe to protect their lead. They don't like risk. They prefer to put their money in safe places, even if they have to accept a lower rate of return.

You can usually identify a conservative investor by the investments comprising her portfolio:

- 50 percent or less in equities (of this percentage, no more than 20 percent, and preferably 10 percent or less, in commodities or high-risk equities). The more conservative the person, the lower the portfolio's equity allocation.

- 50 percent or more in lower-risk investments, including treasury bonds, municipal bonds, bank accounts, certificates of deposit, and money market funds.

In general, the older you are, the more conservative you should be because protecting principal takes precedence over earning huge profits. This guideline is especially true the closer you are to retirement because you have less time to recover from a severe market crash.

Aggressive

Aggressive investors go for the gold, pursuing investments with higher rates of return. Because of this, a higher percentage of the investments in their portfolios is allocated to riskier investments:

- ✔ 70 percent or more in equities or other riskier assets

- ✔ 30 percent or less in lower-risk investments, including treasury bonds, municipal bonds, bank accounts, certificates of deposit, and money market funds

The classic definition of an aggressive investor is someone comfortable in taking on large amounts of risk. The longer you have to recover from a market correction, the more aggressive you can afford to be. Young people in their 20s and 30s can afford to be the most aggressive because they have the time to recover from significant losses.

Many aggressive investors hold commodities, such as gold or silver, stocks from emerging markets in Asia or Africa, or junk bonds from companies with poor credit.

Formulating an Investment Plan

You don't set out on vacation and then plan for it. That would be absurd. Yet this mindset is the equivalent of what many misdirected investors do: They start investing before they even have a destination or goal in mind, let alone a plan or a budget. Not knowing where they're going or how they plan to get there, they waste a lot of time and money trying to find their way.

To avoid this headache, you first need to ask yourself whether you really want to be an investor. If you plan on living fast and dying young, you should probably just spend all your money. Not to be too morbid, but if that's your plan, you have no reason to save your pennies for a rainy day. Carpe diem!

However, if you have any thoughts of longevity, building a family, and retiring, you should start saving money now. In the following sections, I assist you in defining your investment goals, developing a viable plan, and making sure all the pieces are in place before you set out on your journey.

Defining your goals

Most people have a goal in mind before they start investing. They want to save money to buy a home, finance their children's education, retire in comfort, or start their own business. When defining your investment goal, consider two things: the amount of money you need and when you need it. Then choose a time frame that best fits your goal:

- ✔ **Short-term:** *Short-term goals* include buying a new vehicle, taking a nice vacation, renovating a home, or paying off a debt.

- ✔ **Intermediate-term:** *Intermediate-term goals* may include saving for a down payment on a house, traveling the world for a year, or financing a new business venture.

- ✔ **Long-term:** *Long-term goals* are beyond the foreseeable future (about five years out) and include things such as paying for a child's college education or retiring while continuing the lifestyle that you're accustomed to.

A comfortable retirement should be everyone's number one long-term goal. Stocks provide a great place for investing toward long-term goals because they need a long time horizon to maximize returns while minimizing risk.

Putting a plan in place

After you have a goal in mind, you have two points: where you are now and where you want to be when you reach your destination. Your next job is to develop a plan that moves you from point A to point B within your pre-established time frame without derailing the train.

One of the best ways to determine how much money you need to invest toward reaching your goal is to play what-if with a financial calculator. You can find financial calculators all over the Web. Using a simple investment goal calculator, like the one from AARP (`www.aarp.org/money/toolkit/articles/investment_goal_calculator.html`), you can play with the following numbers to determine how much you need to invest per month to achieve your goal:

- ✔ **Investment goal:** The total amount of money you need.

- ✔ **Number of years to accumulate:** Your time frame.

- ✔ **Amount of initial investment:** The initial amount you plan on investing, if any.

- ✔ **Periodic contribution:** The amount you plan on contributing on a regular basis.

- ✔ **Investment frequency:** How often you plan on making a periodic contribution; for example, monthly or quarterly.

- ✔ **Rate of return on investment:** The percentage return you realistically expect from your investments per year.

- ✔ **Expected inflation rate:** The average inflation rate over the time frame in which you plan on investing.

- ✔ **Interest is compounded:** Whether the returns on your investment are compounded, and if so, how frequently (monthly, quarterly, or annually).

- ✔ **Tax rates:** Federal and state tax rates on your dividends and any capital gains.

Even more common on the Web are short-term investment calculators. You simply plug in the current cost of whatever you want to purchase, the inflation rate for that item, your time frame (in years), your state and federal tax rate on your dividends or capital gains, and the percentage yield you expect from your investment, and the calculator determines how much money you need to invest today to reach your goal.

 "Pay yourself first" is cliché for financial advisors, but it's the best strategy for achieving financial goals on time. After setting your goals, make sure you're setting aside enough money each month (or each payday) to achieve those goals according to the time frame you set. For more about financial goal setting, see *Personal Finance For Dummies* (Wiley), by Eric Tyson.

Budgeting to stay on course

After you've established how much money you need to invest to reach your financial goal, develop a budget to cover the rest of your expenses. Otherwise, you're likely to overspend on living expenses, which can put your entire investment plan in jeopardy.

Careful budgeting can help you achieve your investment goals sooner. By trimming the fat from your household budget, you may find that you have more money to invest.

A detailed budget lists all income and expense categories. For example, you may have income from one or more jobs along with investment and interest income. Your expenses may include groceries, rent or a mortgage payment, taxes, auto fuel and maintenance, insurance, utilities, gifts, entertainment, dining, and even personal items. Be sure to include, as an expense, the money you're setting aside for investments. If your budget is in the black, good for you. If it's in the red, you need to start trimming your expenses or looking for an additional (or better-paying) job.

Start using a personal finance program, such as Quicken, to track your income and expenses. When recording transactions, you can assign them to specific categories, including Groceries, Utilities, Automobile, Gifts, Dining, and so on. These programs can help you develop a budget and generate reports that clearly show whether you've been overspending in a particular category.

Planning Specifically for Retirement

Planning for retirement is often more complex than simply setting a goal and using a single, solitary investment vehicle to reach it. You may need to account for money from several sources, including Social Security, a pension, a company's 401(k) plan, and your own individual retirement account (IRA). Through some of these accounts, the federal government encourages citizens to invest for retirement and provides some tax incentives for doing so.

In the following sections, I point out the various types of accounts you may be able to rely on for retirement income so that you can take into consideration all likely sources of income and discount some sources you'd be better off *not* relying on.

Consult a tax expert when planning for retirement so that you can take full advantage of the federal government's tax incentives. By paying less income tax on your earnings, you may be able to afford investing more to reach your retirement goals much sooner.

Because Social Security and pensions aren't guaranteed in the end, the only money you can count on for retirement is the money you bring into your household. Whatever you don't spend today may be all you have to live on later. Be wise about how much you spend and how you invest the money you earn.

Social Security

Social Security is a federal social-insurance program with a variety of benefits, including providing retirement income. Developed in 1935, it became a cornerstone of President Franklin D. Roosevelt's New Deal created to pull the United States out of the Great Depression. The program bases your retirement income on the average wage you earned over your working life. You can begin collecting retirement benefits as young as 62 years or wait until the age of 67 to qualify for significantly higher payments.

If the Social Security Administration (SSA) isn't already keeping you posted about your estimated retirement benefits, contact it and request a copy of your Social Security statement, which shows how much Social Security income you can expect per month upon retirement. You can visit your local SSA office; call 800-772-1213 (TTY 800-325-0778); or request a copy of your statement online at www.ssa.gov.

Pensions

For a good part of the 20th century, companies in the United States funded pension plans for their workers. The workers didn't need to worry about 401(k)s, IRAs, and all that other complicated stuff because their companies took care of depositing money into the pension fund and hiring a manager to invest the money and make sure enough would be available for retirees.

Unfortunately, those days are long gone. Although a few companies still pay pensions, most of the companies that offered pensions have either eliminated them or been eliminated themselves. Some companies simply mismanaged their pension funds and ran out of money to cover their obligations. Many companies have elected to scale back benefits to avoid running out of money, and some have simply gone out of business or been acquired by other companies that suspended the pension programs.

When planning for retirement, assume you're not going to receive a pension, even if you're scheduled to. If you have a pension, good for you, but you can't count on it paying benefits throughout your retirement. Even historically reliable pension funds have been known to disappear during troubled economic times. By planning for the worst-case scenario, you get an added bonus if you do end up receiving a pension.

Defined contribution plans

The federal government realizes that Social Security may run out of funds to cover retirement benefits. In order to prevent a financial calamity with millions of retirees having no money, the feds have put programs in place to encourage citizens to start saving for retirement. At the center of the government's efforts are tax-deferred retirement savings plans named after numbers, including 401(k), 403(b), and 457.

- ✔ **401(k) plan:** A defined contribution retirement plan provided by a commercial entity

- ✔ **403(b) plan:** The equivalent of a 401(k) plan for nonprofit enterprises such as colleges, school districts, hospitals, and other organizations

- ✔ **457 plan:** A defined contribution plan for employees of state and local governments

Calling a tax-deferred retirement savings plan a 401(k) plan may seem a little weird. It begs the question of what happened to the 400 plan, or the 300 or 200 plan, for that matter. The name comes from paragraph (k) in Section 401 of the Internal Revenue Code. Added in 1978, this arcane passage explains in detail how the plans work. Collectively, the 401(k), 403(b), and 457 plans are referred to as *defined contribution*

plans. In the battle of nomenclature, pensions are now called *defined benefit plans.* Unlike a defined benefit plan, which a company provides for you, you contribute the money in defined contribution plans.

The key benefit of the defined contribution plan, other than a nice retirement nest egg, is that you can invest pretax dollars, so presumably you have more money to invest. For example, if you earn $100, you can invest all of it instead of having to pay $25 in federal income tax (leaving you with only $75 to invest). The major disadvantages to defined contribution plans are the limitations on how much you can invest each year and the narrow selection of investment opportunities offered. Some 401(k) plans offer the opportunity to buy stocks, but most plans offer you a limited selection of mutual funds you probably would never buy on your own.

Some employers offer matching contributions; for example, they may contribute 50 cents or even a dollar for every dollar you invest up to a certain annual dollar amount. This setup allows you two ways to build your nest egg much more quickly: by investing pretax dollars and collecting matching contributions. If your employer offers matching contributions, try to take full advantage.

If the option is available, I recommend that you manage your own fund. Of course you don't have complete control. You're restricted to investing in only the options available inside the plan and probably don't have the option of buying individual stocks. However, the more control you have over the fund, the more control you have over the outcome.

Accounts you create yourself

All the accounts I mention in the preceding sections can help you achieve your financial goals. But with the exception of the rare 401(k) plan, none of those plans gives you the freedom to invest as much as you want in anything you want. The only place you can execute a dividend-stock strategy exactly to your specifications is in an account you set up. Your choices include an Individual Retirement Account (IRA), Roth IRA, Keogh, and a taxable account set up at a brokerage firm.

✔ **Individual Retirement Account (IRA):** An IRA is a tax-deferred retirement savings account; that is, you pay taxes only when you withdraw money, so you contribute tax-deferred dollars and your investment grows tax-free. Assuming you earn less than a specified amount and don't belong to an employer-sponsored retirement plan, such as a 401(k), the government allows you to deduct from your income taxes the annual contribution to the account. You can set up an IRA at a bank or brokerage.

To use your IRA to invest in dividend stocks, set up the IRA with a discount broker.

IRAs do have limitations. Currently, the maximum annual tax-deductible contribution is $5,500 for people younger than 50 years of age and $6,500 for people older than 50. The restrictions on how much you can earn to qualify for an IRA and the contribution amounts change often, so contact the people where you set up the account to get the current details.

✔ **Roth IRA:** Like an IRA, the Roth IRA offers some tax benefits. Unlike an IRA, you pay your taxes on the money going in and withdraw it tax-free on the way out. Assuming you take more money out than you put in, the Roth IRA actually offers a better tax break.

✔ **Keogh account:** Similar to an IRA but exclusively for the self-employed, this tax-deferred account allows you to deduct much higher contributions from your taxable income. Like the IRA, the withdrawals are taxed as ordinary income, but you're allowed to invest much more in pretax dollars.

✔ **Brokerage account:** The brokerage account offers the most freedom but no tax benefits. You can invest as much as you want into anything you want — no restrictions. However, every year your earnings are subject to capital gains and/or dividend taxes, so your investment can't benefit from tax-deferred growth. See Chapter 10 for more about setting up a brokerage account.

Chapter 8

Risky Business: Assessing Risk and Your Risk Tolerance

···

In This Chapter

▶ Recognizing the tradeoffs between risk and reward

▶ Estimating and beefing up your risk tolerance

▶ Addressing factors that often increase risk

▶ Acquiring a few techniques for minimizing risk

···

*L*ife is a risk. In fact, most things people find worthwhile are risky: driving, flying, swimming, getting married, raising kids, starting a business, or buying a house. But people often engage in these activities because the reward (or at least the promise of reward) is worth the risk.

We all have a different *risk tolerance,* a threshold beyond which we won't willingly venture. Some people draw the line at public speaking. For others, it's bungee jumping, whitewater rafting, or sealing themselves in a barrel to take a thrill ride down Niagara Falls. Investing is risky too, but you get to choose the level of risk and can take steps to reduce your exposure to it.

In this chapter, you discover how to measure risk and reward, gain a deeper understanding of the tradeoffs, gauge your level of risk tolerance, recognize the factors that can increase risk, and pick up a few techniques for improving your odds.

In investing, the riskier the investment, the greater the potential for big returns or big losses.

Weighing Risk and Reward

Barron's calls *risk* the measurable possibility of losing money. It's different from *uncertainty,* which isn't measurable. *Reward,* of course, is what you stand to gain if your risk pays off. Investors have a couple ways of measuring risk and reward. I use these methods in the following sections to demonstrate how risks and rewards generally interact in terms of investments.

Graphing risk versus reward

One way to gain a sense of how risk and reward generally play out in the world of investing is to look at a graph such as Figure 8-1 that shows how investments with different relative risk levels perform over time (this figure compares stocks, bonds, and cash with inflation from 1987 through 2007). Note the following types of investment vehicles:

- **Cash:** Parking your money in the bank or a money-market fund may seem pretty safe, but you can expect a return that's significantly lower than that for stocks and bonds and may not even keep pace with inflation.

- **Bonds:** By investing in bonds, you retain some security while enhancing the potential return on your investment.

- **Stocks:** Stock prices rise and fall, but when all is said and done, they generally provide you with an opportunity for a significantly higher rate of return. As I explain in Chapter 3, dividend stocks offer greater stability while still enabling you to score the higher returns stocks offer.

Time can be your friend or foe. Young investors can take more risks than older investors because they can afford to spend some time waiting until the market recovers before withdrawing their money. Older investors are generally advised to play it safe and protect the gains they've earned over their many years, because soon they'll need to cash out their chips.

© John Wiley & Sons, Inc.

Figure 8-1: Riskier investments tend to produce higher returns over time.

Assigning a number to investment risk

Assigning a number or a risk level to various endeavors can be quite a challenge. I suppose on a scale of one to ten, taking a nap would rank one and rock climbing may rank nine or ten. Investors have a much more precise measure of risk: *volatility,* which is the range in which an investment generally moves.

Calculating volatility is a task best suited for mathematicians. I mention it here only to make you aware that highly volatile investments are generally riskier than those that sail on a more even keel.

Fortunately, stocks that pay dividends are generally much less volatile than pure growth stocks.

Assigning a number to rewards

Assigning a number to investment rewards is easy: It's a dollar amount or a percentage. All you have to do is look at your statements.

- ✔ A positive number indicates reward. The bigger the number, the greater the reward.

- ✔ A negative number means you've just been spanked. Hey, it happens to the best of us.

Recognizing the risk of no risk

If you lie in bed all day doing nothing, your risk of not living a full life is 100 percent. The same is true when you're dealing with money. If you don't take some risk with it, it loses value. Unless you invest it in something that provides a decent return, inflation gnaws away at it with each passing day.

To protect your savings, put your money to work by investing it in something that offers a return at least equal to the inflation rate.

Remain aware of the risk of not taking a risk. It's one sure way to lose money.

Gauging and Raising Your Risk Tolerance

Before you send your money out in the world to earn profits for you, you need to determine how worried you're going to be about it. How much risk can you tolerate without getting sick over it?

How you perceive risks and respond to losses is very personal and not something you can assign a number to. However, you can gauge your risk tolerance to gain a clearer understanding of the types of investments you feel comfortable with. You can also stretch your comfort zone by adjusting your perspective. The following sections show you how.

Measuring risk tolerance in sleepless nights

You don't want to lose sleep over your investments, so try gauging your risk tolerance in relation to sleepless nights. Use the following guidelines to estimate your comfort level:

- ✓ **High tolerance:** You can handle extreme volatility in your investments and the possibility of massive losses, and you're able to sleep at night when the market is in turmoil.

✔ **Average tolerance:** You can handle average-sized drops in price for extended periods, but the extreme stuff makes you anxious, jumpy, and unable to sleep at night.

✔ **Low tolerance:** Losses of 5 percent keep you awake at night. It's mostly bonds and bank accounts for you. Don't lose faith though. You may be able to expand your comfort zone, as I cover in the following section.

Boosting your risk tolerance with the promise of rewards

Whenever you're thinking about investing in anything, consider the potential rewards along with the risks to determine whether taking the chance is worth it to you. Risk tolerance isn't set in stone. The levels of risk and reward influence your decision. If a complete stranger presents you with an opportunity to risk $10,000 to earn a buck, you're going to tell the guy to take a hike. On the other hand, if someone you trust completely in financial matters assures you that investing $10,000 will earn you $20,000 by the end of the year (and you have an extra ten grand sitting in the bank), you'd probably jump at the offer.

Table 8-1 provides some guidelines to help you decide whether a particular level of risk is right for you.

Table 8-1	Risk/Reward Guidelines
Risk Level	*Reward Level*
High	Potential for high returns or losses
Average	High potential for average returns or losses, but still a little potential for high returns or losses
Low	High probability of small returns or losses, average potential for average returns or losses, and very little potential for high returns or losses

Don't risk what you can't afford to lose. If you've saved $20,000 to send your daughter to college next year, investing in stocks, even "safe" stocks recommended by a trusted source, is probably a bad idea. If your share prices drop, you have little or no time to recover from the losses before you need to cash out.

Recognizing Factors That Can Increase Risk

Risk is ever present, but it's always variable and unpredictable. Although you can't eliminate risk, you can often reduce your exposure to it by becoming more aware of the factors that influence it.

Risk factors you can control

Even the riskiest activities offer ways for participants to reduce the risk. For example, skydivers can pack their own parachutes. Racecar drivers can strap themselves in and wear helmets. In much the same way, investors mitigate their risks by dealing with factors they can control.

Reducing human error

Human error is the biggest risk factor with investing, and it can come in many forms:

- Insufficient knowledge
- Lack of research and analysis
- Choosing the wrong investment strategy for your goals
- Failure to monitor market conditions
- Choosing stocks emotionally rather than rationally (see the following section)
- Letting fear and panic influence investment decisions

The best way to remove human error from the equation is to do your homework. If you've ever taken an exam you haven't studied for, you know the risk involved in not being prepared.

Investing less emotionally

Don't let emotions govern your investment decisions. Remain particularly cautious of the following emotions:

- **Greed:** Greed often seduces investors into making terrible decisions. During market rallies, investors often succumb to a herd mentality, throwing their money into the hottest sectors and companies, inflating a bubble that invariably bursts. Greedy investors often tend to make bets they can't afford to lose and then fall into the trap of making even bigger bets to recover their losses.

✔ **Fear:** Fear is the flip side of greed. People who previously lost money in the market, or just witnessed the pain felt by others, can experience such a massive fear of losing money that it paralyzes them from doing anything. Instead of taking on some risk with suitable investments, they put their money in low-risk investments with poor rates of return.

✔ **Love:** Don't fall in love with your investments. They don't return your love but have a good chance of hurting and betraying you. When a stock falls sharply on very bad news, you need to bail out. Remember, you're not married to a stock. On a regular basis, look at your stocks and ask them, "What have you done for me lately?" If the answer doesn't satisfy you, you can unceremoniously dump them without hurting anyone's feelings.

Spreading your nest eggs among several baskets

Regardless of how promising a company is, you should never invest all your money in it. Management may be incompetent or corrupt. Competitors may claim more market share. Or the company or its entire sector can lose investors' favor for whatever reason.

The good news is that you have total control over where you invest your money. You can significantly reduce your risk by spreading it out through *diversification.* See "Mitigating Your Risks" later in this chapter for details.

Factors outside your control

You can't always control what happens around you. Inflation can soar, the Federal Reserve can decide to raise or lower interest rates, bubbles can burst, and entire economies can crumble. However, by becoming more aware of these risks, you can develop strategies for dealing with them effectively.

Beating inflation

Inflation is a silent killer, eating away at your savings unless you put that money to work by investing it in something that earns a higher rate of return than the rate of inflation. And it's worse than most people realize.

An inflation rate of 4 percent means that something that cost a dollar last year costs $1.04 this year. If your yearly expenses total $40,000 this year, next year you'll have to spend $41,600 to buy the same amount of groceries, clothing, gas, and everything else. The year after that, those same goods and services will cost $43,264. If your salary doesn't keep up and your investments don't make enough to cover the distance, you will have to dig into your savings to make up the difference.

Dividend stocks provide a great way to offset inflation risk. Buying dividend stocks that yield as much as the rate of inflation keeps you even in terms of what your money can buy. Any stock price appreciation is pure profit. Buy stocks with dividends greater than inflation, and you always see your money grow in real terms.

Adjusting to interest rate hikes

When the Federal Reserve hikes interest rates, it hurts companies in a variety of ways, which can have a significant effect on dividends:

- ✔ **Interest rate hikes increase costs and slash the bottom line.** With a higher interest rate, a company that carries a high debt load must pay more the next time it borrows funds. This jump increases its cost of doing business, which may hurt the company's profitability and trigger a drop in share price.

- ✔ **Rising rates hurt business-to-business sales.** When companies are spending more to service their debt, they have less money to purchase goods and services from suppliers. Everyone suffers.

- ✔ **Stocks become less attractive.** When interest rates rise, safer investments earn a higher rate of return. If the yield on a bond or money market account equals the yield on a stock but carries a lot less risk, many investors sell their shares and move into bonds to maximize returns while lowering risk. This switch can send stock prices lower.

Investing in dividend stocks provides some protection against interest rate hikes. Even if the share price drops, companies often continue paying dividends, which offset the drop in price.

Steering clear of companies with fuzzy financials

In the stock market, you can lose all your money if the companies you invest in go belly up or post significant losses.

You can often avoid making mistakes by carefully researching the companies you plan to buy. At the very least, you need to look at a company's financial statements to see whether earnings and revenues are growing or falling. For more about evaluating dividend stocks, see Chapter 9.

Monitoring market risk

Market crashes are a fact of life. The main way to mitigate this risk is the same as for financial risk: research. Invest in good, profitable, stable companies because they tend to weather the storm better than most.

Riding out a slumping economy

Like the stock market, the economy has its ups and downs. In fact, the stock market typically reflects current economic conditions. And, generally speaking, what's bad for the economy is bad for the stock market.

As a dividend investor, you can't control the economy or prevent an economic meltdown, but you can mitigate your losses and often gain ground in a slumping economy. Remember that a drop in share prices just may signal a perfect buying opportunity.

Reacting to changes in the tax code

The federal government often tries to influence consumer behavior and business practices through tax code. As a voter, you have some control over the tax code, but not much. You have more control over developing an investment strategy that takes advantage of favorable changes and protects your investments against unfavorable changes.

Adjusting to shifts in government policy

Although the stock market is filled with uncertainty, it does have a certain amount of predictability. When the government intervenes, however, predictability is tossed out the window. Yes, the United States does have a free market economy, but the government often steps in to influence it. And when the government steps in, the effects tend to ripple through the markets.

You may not be able to control or even predict changes in government policy, but it's a good idea to keep up on the news and try to understand how specific policies or even talk of policy changes may affect your share prices and investment strategy. In addition, a slow, steady approach to investing can help reduce the effects of policy changes on your portfolio.

Remaining aware of credit risk

Keep in mind that banks aren't risk-free either. They may seem safe, at least until *credit risk* (the risk of a loss caused by failure to pay) rears its head. A bank can fail to have enough cash to meet capital requirements, essentially owing more than it owns. This situation can cause a bank to collapse, and as the crash of 2008 demonstrated, collapsing banks aren't just a historical phenomenon.

Mitigating Your Risks

You can never completely eliminate risk. Whether you choose to invest your money or not, you always risk losing at least some of it. You can, however, reduce your exposure to risk by following a sensible plan and doing your homework. The following sections suggest four risk-reduction techniques employed by the pros.

Matching your strategy to your time frame

One of the easiest ways to lose a significant chunk of change in the stock market is to make risky investments. An even easier way is to make risky investments when you have insufficient time to recover from any drop in share price. In other words, if you buy some shares, they drop in price, and you *have to* sell because you need the cash right now, you're going to lose money.

Choose investments according to your time frame. If you're young and can afford to leave your money in the market, you can also afford to take on more risk for the promise of bigger returns. If, on the other hand, you're going to need that money sometime in the near future, play it safe.

Performing your due diligence

Novice investors, and some greedy pros, attempt to ride the waves of investor enthusiasm by purchasing popular stocks. This practice is certainly okay if the company's fundamentals justify the share price. It's never okay if shares are way over-valued compared to the company's earnings and its realistic growth projections. You can significantly reduce your risks by carefully researching companies before investing in them.

Diversifying your investments

Diversification is just a fancy way of saying "Don't put all your eggs in one basket." It's one of the best ways to protect your portfolio from the many forms of risk. Diversification demands that you hold many different asset classes in your portfolio to spread the risk. (*Assets* are any items of value. An *asset class* is a group of similar assets.) With this strategy, a significant loss in any one investment or class doesn't destroy your entire portfolio. More importantly, it ensures that in the event of a loss, you retain at least some capital to make future investments — and hopefully recover what you lost.

Analysts often use the concept of correlation to guide their diversification decisions. *Correlation* determines how closely two assets follow each other as they bounce up and down on the charts. Analysts measure correlation on a scale from 1 to –1. The number 1 represents *perfect correlation,* and –1 represents *perfect inverse correlation.* For instance, when oil prices rise, nearly all the oil companies rise together, achieving perfect or near perfect correlation. When oil rises 10 percent, but automobile companies lose 10 percent, their relationship represents perfect inverse correlation. A correlation of 0 (zero) means the rise and fall of any two sectors or stocks are unrelated.

To diversify, follow a process of asset allocation. Populate your portfolio with a variety of asset classes with different degrees of correlation, such as stocks, bonds, commodities, mutual funds, or ETFs.

Employing dollar cost averaging

Dollar cost averaging is a disciplined investment strategy that, over time, can prevent you from paying too much for shares. Here's how it works: You buy a certain fixed dollar amount of shares regularly — say every month, quarter, or year. As a result, you end up buying more shares when the price is low and fewer shares when the price is high, but you don't get stuck buying all of your shares at the higher price. Therefore, the price you pay is a reasonable average.

Chapter 9

Choosing Your Approach — And Your Dividends

....

....

*T*he stock market is really big. How big depends on when you measure, what you use to measure it, and who's doing the measuring. On October 31, 2007, the Dow Jones U.S. Total Stock Market Index, which contains all U.S. equities that have readily available prices, held 4,875 stocks valued at $18.9 trillion. By December 2009, it held 4,209 stocks and its value had plunged 30 percent to $13.2 trillion. Thousands more trade over the counter (OTC), where stocks for newer and smaller companies are more likely to be traded.

Any way you count 'em, that's a lot of stocks to sift through to find a few nuggets of gold, even if you scratch non-dividend stocks off your list. Fortunately, several resources are available to help investors screen out the poorest prospects and focus on only the most promising candidates. In this chapter, I tell you about approaches to investing and then reveal useful tools for tracking down potentially good dividend stocks.

Finding the Right Investing Approach for You

The goal of every investor is to make money. As with most things in life, several paths lead to the same destination. When you're an investor, you can make money through any of the approaches I discuss in this section: growth investing, income investing, value investing, or a combination.

The dividend investing approach I recommend combines the best of all three of these methods, starting with income. After identifying some stocks with acceptable yields, you can begin to search for bargains that offer a good potential for both price appreciation and dividends.

The growth approach

With *growth investing,* you buy stocks in companies with earnings and revenue growth rates that exceed the market average in anticipation of big jumps in the share price; these stocks are typically young or small companies that reinvest their earnings to maximize growth and typically don't pay dividends. Growth investors are like scouts for professional sports. Their job is to evaluate the up and coming talent and identify the most promising athletes. Growth investors want to see companies with potential — companies that are growing faster than the competition and other companies in their industry. They're interested in companies that plow every penny of profit back into the company to fuel future growth. Because of this focus, growth investors care little or nothing about dividends.

Don't confuse growth with share price appreciation. Growth is a measure of a company's earnings and revenue increases relative to similar companies. Share price merely reflects what investors are willing to pay for the stock, which may have nothing to do with the company's actual performance.

Growth stocks get their moniker if their earnings and revenues grow at a faster pace than their particular end of the market. For instance, a large-cap stock growing at a faster rate than the S&P 500 is considered a growth stock. Small-cap stocks have to show a greater growth rate than the index for the small-cap market, the Russell 2000, to be considered growth stocks.

Large-cap is short for large market capitalization. Small-cap is the abbreviation for small market capitalization. Market capitalization is a fancy phrase for a company's market value, determined by multiplying its share price by its number of outstanding common shares. The definitions aren't set in stone, but currently, a large market cap is greater than $10 billion. A small market cap is between $300 million and $2 billion.

Because the focus is on growth, certain measures, including a company's price-to-earnings ratio or price-to-sales ratio carry less weight. Growth investors are more concerned with how the company did this quarter compared with how it performed in the quarter 12 months earlier. Here's the formula:

Growth Rate = (This Year's Profit − Last Year's Profit) ÷ Last Year's Profit

For example, say Dubois Foods earned $1 million last year and $1.25 million this year:

($1.25 million − $1 million) ÷ $1 million = 25 percent

Growth investors generally evaluate growth stocks based on the following criteria:

✔ **Earnings and revenue growth rates higher than the broader market and other companies in the same industry:** Growth rates should be at least 10 percent. If the earnings growth rate is faster than the revenue growth rate, the company is also keeping costs down.

✔ **Consistent growth rate for several consecutive years:** A one-year jump is a fluke. Five years of consistent growth is a trend.

Growth investors aren't scared by P/E (price-to-earnings) ratios in the 20s, 30s, and 40s, which means the price of each share is 20, 30, or even 40 times higher than each share is earning. If the earnings are growing fast enough, the price is warranted.

Comparing this year's results to last year's results provides the annual growth rate, but what if you're in the end of the third quarter? Over nine months, a lot can change. Are those numbers still relevant? The most recent growth rate compares the most recent fiscal quarter to the same fiscal quarter last year. The reason you compare the current quarter to the *year-ago* quarter is that business can be cyclical. Ice cream shops sell a lot more in the summer than the winter. So comparing this summer quarter to the year-ago summer quarter gives you a better comparison of a company's growth because business conditions should be similar.

The income approach

The *income investing* approach encourages you to buy investments, such as stocks or bonds, that promise a steady stream of income; among stock investors, income and dividend investing are one and the same. For most of history, investing was income investing. Whether investing in stocks or bonds, in small or large businesses, investors needed income from their investments to cover their daily expenses. They simply didn't have the surplus cash on hand to let it sit in the market for several years until they could sell and reap their profit.

When you're investing for income and looking for a relatively safe and steady cash flow, you have several options (in addition to investing in dividend stocks). These options include ranging savings accounts, money market accounts, certificates of deposit (CDs), and bonds.

The main attraction of most conservative, income-investing options like the one's I've listed is that they help protect your principal — when the game is over, you can expect to walk away with at least as much money as you started.

When you're focused on income investing, particularly through dividend stocks, three criteria step into the spotlight:

- ✔ **Yield** is the percentage return on your investment you see exclusively from dividends. If you buy shares for $20 each and the company pays $2 per share for the year, the yield is 10 percent: $2 ÷ $20 = 10 percent. When you're investing solely for income, make sure the yield is greater than the inflation rate; for example, if inflation is at 3 percent, eliminate most stocks yielding less than 4 percent.

✔ **Payout ratio** is the percentage of its profits a company pays out as a dividend to shareholders. Anything over 50 percent is good. Most companies pay between 50 and 75 percent. Higher is usually better, but anything more than 100 percent is a red flag because it means the money is coming from someplace other than profits.

✔ **Dividend growth** demonstrates a company's ability to earn ever-increasing profits and share ever-increasing dividends with shareholders. Dividend growth is just as important as, if not more important than, yield. A low-yielding stock with a steady stream of increases may be a better investment than a high-yielding stock that hasn't increased the dividend in years.

For all the extra risk you accept with the purchase of dividend stocks, you receive a huge benefit: the potential for income growth from a steadily increasing dividend. This advantage can be more important than a high yield because every time the dividend increases, the yield on your initial investment increases. If you buy a $10 stock with an annual dividend of 20 cents, you receive a 2 percent yield. If the company increases the dividend by a nickel every year, after four years the yield on your initial investment will have doubled to 4 percent.

The value approach

In a *value investing* approach, you buy stocks with steady profit streams selling at prices below their true market value. Value investors search for *underappreciated* stocks: companies with a total stock value lower than the value of the shareholder equity, also known as working capital. These stocks are typically well-established companies that pay dividends, especially companies way down in price compared to their historical average share price. The more beaten-down the stock's price, the better the value.

On the stock market, supply and demand generally rule the roost. As a result, a stock's worth at any given point in time is determined by whatever investors are willing to pay for it. The key to value investing is to follow a less biased and less emotional approach in estimating the true value of a stock.

✔ According to *Efficient Market Theory,* you can't possibly gain an advantage over other investors because investors are rational and all of them have access to the same information. In other words, you may as well just buy an index fund.

✔ *Fundamental Analysis* basically asserts that the Efficient Market Theory is a bunch of hooey. Although the market may be efficient on a yearly basis, it sure isn't on a daily, weekly, monthly, or quarterly basis. Value investors are fundamental analysts. They analyze a company's past results to evaluate its current financial health and then to predict the company's future growth in earnings, revenues, and stock price.

Although past results are certainly no guarantee of future performance, past performance can be a good *predictor* of future performance. A company with a proven history of good management, innovation, and revenue and earnings growth can be expected to continue along that path until experiencing a drastic change.

Dividend-paying growth stocks at bargain prices

Value, income, and growth aren't mutually exclusive. Even growth investors are looking for bargains, and all investors are ultimately trying to score some income. No investor is going to pass up a true bargain.

The sweet spot of stock investing occurs when you find a company exhibiting characteristics of all three approaches: a hot stock at a cheap price.

When shopping for stocks, use all three criteria to narrow the field. You can start by looking for dividend stocks with a minimum acceptable yield (for example, 1 or 2 percent higher than the current inflation rate) and then screen for growth and value. Or start by searching for undervalued stocks and then screening your list for candidates that meet or exceed your minimum acceptable yield. When you find a stock that meets all of your criteria, you have a true gem that embodies all the positive characteristics of a dividend stock:

- ✔ Steady income stream
- ✔ Good management
- ✔ Fiscal discipline
- ✔ Earnings transparency
- ✔ Dividends increases

Plus the benefits of growth:

- ✔ Strong earnings growth
- ✔ Strong revenue growth

With a steady income stream from dividends and good potential for capital appreciation from growth, you've found a real bargain that promises to limit your exposure to risk while maximizing your profit potential.

 Don't automatically eliminate small-yield stocks. If a company is managed well and demonstrates consistent growth, chances are pretty good it will eventually start increasing its dividend payments. Once it makes that commitment, it's very likely to increase dividend payments on a regular basis.

Sizing Up Potential Picks

On Wall Street perhaps more than anywhere else, knowledge is power, which is why insider trading is illegal — insiders know way too much to play a fair game. As an outsider, however, you want to know as much about the industry, the company, and its stock as possible so you can make a wise purchase decision, maximize your return, and minimize your exposure to risk.

This section shows you how to perform your due diligence so you have the information you need to keep from getting burned by your neighbor's hot tip. Not all dividend stocks are created equal, and the more you know about a company, the better you can judge whether it will continue to pay dividends and how likely it will be to increase its dividend payments.

Key facts and figures

Publicly traded companies are required by law to publish reports — sort of like report cards — that tell current and prospective investors how well (or not so well) the company is doing. The most important of these reports are the following:

- ✔ **Annual Report:** Public companies send this attractive, colorful publication to all of their shareholders once a year. It contains many of the company's year-end financial statements as well as a chronicle of the company's activities during the previous year.

- ✔ **10-K Form:** Similar to the annual report, the *10-K* contains the same financial statements plus a bit more, such as how much the executives get paid and how much stock they own. The Securities and Exchange Commission (SEC) requires companies to file this comprehensive financial statement within 60 days after the end of the company's fiscal year.

- ✔ **10-Q Form:** This document is a quarterly report (hence the *Q*) that contains a company's financial statements, a discussion from management, and a list of "material events" that have occurred during the previous quarter. The SEC requires companies to file a 10-Q within 35 days after the end of each of the first three fiscal quarters. The 10-K contains the fourth-quarter along with the annual results.

- ✔ **8-K Form:** The *8-K* reports any significant events and/ or material changes not made in the ordinary course of business. These material events include a change in auditors, the resignation or election of a director, the completion of asset acquisition or disposition, a bankruptcy, and other material impairments and must be reported within four days of their occurrence.

Don't ignore the most recent 8-Ks. These have potential to be the most important of all the forms. Depending on the news reported, such as a need to restate earnings, an 8-K can make all the other forms useless.

You can obtain a company's most recent annual report by visiting its website or contacting the company and requesting a copy. The best place to find the 10-K, 10-Q, and 8-K forms are on the SEC's website at www.sec.gov. Companies also typically release their balance sheets and income statements in press releases when they announce their quarterly earnings. You can find press releases on the company's website or on financial websites such as Yahoo! Finance (http://finance.yahoo.com) or Google Finance (www.google.com/finance).

Company fundamentals

When you buy shares in a company, you're not just buying pieces of paper; you're buying ownership of that company. You want to make sure that a company you're thinking about investing in is financially sound and that management seems to have its act together. You make this determination by examining the following three documents:

- ✔ Balance sheet
- ✔ Income statement
- ✔ Cash flow statement

The numbers on these statements are the company's *fundamentals* — things like revenues and expenses. In the following sections, I describe each of these documents in greater detail and show you how to decipher them.

After you understand the fundamentals, you can compare these metrics against others to calculate ratios specific to dividend investing. These calculations help you determine the health of the company and make educated predictions about future appreciation and dividend growth. I give you the lowdown on some of these ratios later in the chapter.

Company reports measure past performance, but a stock's value depends entirely on what people expect it to do in the future. Because of this discrepancy, stock analysis pretty much consists of predicting future performance based on current conditions and past performance. Although past performance is all you have to go on, it's no guarantee of future results. Last year's big winner may be this year's big loser, and vice versa.

The balance sheet

The balance sheet presents a financial snapshot of what the company owns and owes at a single point in time, typically at the end of each quarter. It's essentially a net worth statement for a company. The left or top side of the balance sheet lists everything the company owns: its *assets*, also known as *debits*. The right or lower side lists the claims against the company, called *liabilities* or *credits*, and shareholder equity.

Liabilities may not seem like credits to you, but that's not a typo. In accounting lingo, a credit is a loan. A credit brings cash in that the firm can use to purchase an asset. However, this credit is a liability, a debt that must be paid back at a later date. We use *assets* and *liabilities* as our main terms, so don't worry too much about keeping the debits and credits straight.

It's called a balance sheet because each side must equal the other. Assets equal liabilities plus shareholder equity. In other words, whatever assets aren't being used to pay off the liabilities belong to the shareholders. See the later "Shareholder equity" section for more information.

A company's balance sheet is only one item to consider when deciding where to invest your money. You also need to look at the other facts and figures covered in this chapter, along with how the sector (industry) is doing as a whole and the company's outlook as compared to that of other companies you're investigating.

Assets

Assets are items of value that the company owns. The major components that make up the asset side of the balance sheet include current assets, fixed assets, investments, and intangibles. Here's a breakdown:

- **Current Assets:** All liquid assets, which include cash or anything that can easily be turned into cash, like cash equivalents (highly liquid, short-term investments like bank accounts or U.S. Treasury bills), accounts receivables, and inventory.

- **Investments:** Stocks, bonds, or derivatives. Some are long-term investments, but any investment that can be sold for quick cash goes under current assets.

✔ **Fixed Assets:** Tangible, permanent items necessary for the business to operate. Fixed assets include real estate, buildings, vehicles, and equipment. These assets typically have a long life.

✔ **Intangibles:** Anything that has value but isn't involved in the actual production of the good or service. Intangibles include copyrights, patents, trademarks, licenses, and goodwill.

Together, these items add up to total assets. Ideally, assets create income, which pays for future dividends.

Liabilities

Liabilities are sort of like IOUs. They represent the total cash value of what the company owes to other entities. Liabilities aren't necessarily a bad thing. After all, companies have to spend money to make money. They only become a problem when a company is consistently spending more than it's earning and has no clear and viable strategy to reduce that trend. Here's how liabilities typically break down:

✔ **Current Liabilities:** All short-term debt that must be paid back within the next 12 months, such as accounts payable or long-term debt that will be retired in the next 12 months and its interest payments.

✔ **Long-Term Debt:** Any borrowed money that the company will pay back over a time period longer than 12 months. Long-term debt includes bonds, loans from banks, and mortgages.

✔ **Other Liabilities:** Everything else the company owes.

Add current liabilities to long-term debt and other liabilities to calculate total liabilities.

Shareholder equity

Subtract total liabilities from total assets and you end up with the company's *net worth*, also known as *shareholder equity*, which is the shareholders' ownership stake after all the debts are paid. (That's why stocks are also called equities.)

Common stock, preferred stock, and retained earnings comprise the three major parts of shareholder equity. (See Chapter 2 for details about common and preferred stock.)

These items may not be listed in the annual report or press releases, but they can be found in the 10-Q and 10-K SEC filings I discuss earlier in the chapter. They ultimately determine how much each share receives in dividends:

- ✔ **Common stocks:** The number of common shares outstanding.

- ✔ **Preferred stock:** The number of preferred shares outstanding.

- ✔ **Retained Earnings:** The profits left over after dividends have been paid. Also called *undistributed profits* or *earned surplus,* retained earnings provide the funds to make investments and purchase new assets.

The income statement

The *income statement* (also known as the *profit-and-loss* or *P&L statement*) details all of the company's revenues and expenses: how much the company receives in sales and how much the company spends to make those sales. After all the additions and subtractions, the final tally tells you whether the company earned a profit or suffered a loss and how much. The income statement contains the fundamental equation for every business:

Sales − Expenses = Net Income

A positive net income indicates the company is profitable. Zero means it broke even. A negative number shows the company lost money. That's all pretty straightforward, but the income statement usually contains more detail, covering the following items (among other things):

- ✔ **Revenues:** Total dollar amount brought in from sales. Called the *top line* because it's the top line of the income statement, revenues record the company's total (gross) sales of products and services.

- ✔ **Costs of products sold:** Also called *cost of revenue* and *cost of goods sold,* this figure represents the costs of buying raw materials and producing the finished products.

- ✔ **Gross profit:** Deduct the cost of products sold from the total revenues to arrive at gross profit.

The first benchmark comes right here, the *gross margin* or *profit margin*, also known as the *return on sales*. Divide gross profit by revenues to get profit margin. When it comes to dividend stocks, a profit margin of 50 percent of total revenues keeps me interested. Less that 50 percent and I toss it.

✓ **Selling, general, and administrative expense:** This category includes all costs to maintain the business:

- **Selling costs** include all expenditures to sell the product, such as marketing and travel.

- **Administrative** includes salaries and other services such as accountants and lawyers.

- **General costs** encompass the costs to maintain plants and equipment.

✓ **Operating income:** The difference between gross profit and selling, general, and administrative expenses. Operating income represents the total amount of profits that came from the actual performance of the company's business.

✓ **Earnings before interest, taxes, depreciation, and amortization:** These earnings, often referred to as EBITDA, combine operating income with income from investments.

EBITDA is useful in giving a view to profits before non-cash accounting calculations, such as depreciation and amortization, are deducted. However, EBITDA is not an official number under the Generally Accepted Accounting Principles (GAAP), so it can be manipulated to suit management's goals.

✓ **Interest expense:** The interest paid on debt.

✓ **Non operating income:** Any income that doesn't come from the company's operations, such as the sale of assets or investment income.

✓ **Earnings from continuing operations:** Profits from the company's current businesses.

✓ **Earnings from discontinued operations:** Profits from any businesses the company closed or sold this quarter.

✓ **Net Income:** The true profit after every other possible expense has been paid. The profit is the *bottom line*, because it's the last line on the income statement and what really matters at the end of each quarter.

Another key number to check on the income statement is *earnings per share.* You want to see this number going up rather than down.

Earnings per share and net income are different ways to measure the same thing — profits. If they move in different directions, wonder why. Whenever you notice discrepancies like this one, you need to investigate.

Any time you see a number in parentheses, it means that's a negative number, or outflow of money. If the net income figure is in parenthesis, the company recorded a net loss for the quarter.

Income statements compare the most recent quarter to the same quarter a year earlier. Some businesses are cyclical. For instance, retailers make a lot more money during the winter holidays than the first three months of the year. So, to compare the January-to-March quarter to the October-to-December quarter wouldn't be a fair comparison.

The cash flow statement

The *cash flow statement* is like the company's checkbook register. It records the actual movement of all the cash in the company, showing which activities generated the money coming in and what was actually paid for in that quarter. The balance sheet and income statement summarize *how much,* but the cash flow statement provides more details about *where* the cash came from, *what* it was spent on, and (perhaps most importantly) *whether* the company spent more money than it generated.

The cash flow statement measures the movement of money from three different activities: operations, investments, and financing.

> ✔ **Operating activities:** The cash flow statement starts with the net income from the income statement, making it the top line. It then adds back in *depreciation* (an accounting device in which no actual cash moves), other operating expenses that don't involve cash, and gains from the sale of assets. These items add up to the net cash generated from operating activities

✔ **Investing activities:** Any money spent on the purchase of new assets such as machinery, plants, or land gets classified as a *capital expenditure,* or *CapEx.* These new assets go to the future production of income. Companies invest in capital expenditures to maintain and grow the business. Cash flow from investing activities subtracts capital expenditures from all income generated by these assets.

✔ **Financing activities** records the financing of the company's operations, including the payment of dividends, the sale or purchase of stock, and the net amount the company has borrowed.

Although seeing the change in total cash flow over the time period listed is good, the more important take-away number is called *free cash flow.* Here's the formula:

Free Cash Flow = Net Cash from Operating Activities – Capital Expenditures

Negative free cash flow doesn't automatically mean the company is in trouble. It may be making huge investments for future earnings growth. However, it's not a good sign for the dividend investor. Companies need to have cash on hand to pay dividends. If they don't have enough cash on hand, they need to take on debt to make the payments or simply stop paying dividends. Borrowing funds to pay dividends isn't sustainable, so free cash flow gives a clear look at how secure the dividend is.

Calculating a Dividend's Relative Strength

Whenever you buy something, you want to make sure you're getting a good value for the price — something that's "worth it." Buying watered-down laundry detergent at the dollar store may seem like a good deal, but if it takes an entire bottle to do a single load of laundry, the expensive stuff may actually cost less. Shopping for stocks is no different. You're looking for a good buy, which is a stock whose price values it less than other companies with similar profit-making potential.

After you get a handle on the balance sheet, income statement, and cash flow statement (which I cover in the preceding section), you can start to play around with financial ratios. These simple mathematical equations measure the health of the company and its dividend. In the following sections, I introduce the various equations and show you how to use the results of these equations to perform your very own dividend stock analysis.

Yield

Yield (also known as *dividend yield*) is your dividend's rate of return, and one of the most important numbers to consider. It enables you to compare stocks side-by-side, ensure that a particular stock meets the minimum return requirement for your portfolio, and avoid stocks that have comparatively high dividends (in dollars) but low returns (in percentage).

Don't confuse dividend with dividend yield. The cold, hard cash that lands in your pocket every quarter is the dividend. Yield is the annual percentage return in dividends on your investment.

Yield is a huge consideration for two reasons:

- ✔ It indicates the minimum rate of return you can expect to earn on your shares.

- ✔ It determines whether you can expect this investment to beat inflation. If inflation is running at 3 percent and the yield is only 2.5 percent, you stand to lose ½ percent per year to inflation. (Of course, if the share price rises, too, your return may still beat inflation.)

Use the following guidelines to gauge the relative attractiveness of a stock based on its yield:

- ✔ **Low yield:** Less than the average yield on the S&P 500 Index. The minimum return of low-yield stocks increases your risk because the dividend provides a smaller buffer should the shares drop in price and may fail to keep up with the market or rate of inflation.

However, don't automatically rule out low-yield stocks. A low-yield stock with consistently rising payouts may turn out to be a better investment than a medium-yield stock with static payouts. If the low-yield dividend grows on a consistent basis, that increases the yield on your original investment, which may soon be higher than the yield of both the market and the stock with the static dividend. In addition, low-yield stocks are often growth companies with the potential for above-average gains in share price.

✔ **Medium yield:** Between the S&P 500 yield and up to three percentage points more than the index's yield.

✔ **High yield:** More than three percentage points higher than the yield on the S&P 500.

Calculating dividend per share

To calculate yield, you must first calculate *dividend per share* — the amount of money you receive each quarter for each share of stock you own. The easiest way to "calculate" this number is to look at the income statement and find the number next to "Dividends per Share." If the number isn't easily available, the calculation is pretty straightforward:

Dividend per Share = Total Dividends ÷ Total Shares

To find the total dividends the company paid, look at the company's cash flow statement under the heading "Financing Activities."

A small dividend-per-share isn't necessarily bad, nor is a large dividend-per-share necessarily good. The relevant number here is yield — the rate of return on your investment. A small dividend per share on a low-priced stock may be better than a big dividend on high-priced stock.

Computing the indicated dividend per share

Although the dividend per share is important, it represents only the quarterly dividend. To get the annual yield, you need the *indicated dividend,* also called the *annual dividend per share,* because this dividend "indicates" the yield.

The calculation is easy as pie:

Indicated Dividend = Quarterly Dividend per Share × 4

You may need to adjust the equation if the company pays dividends on a nonstandard schedule. Some companies pay monthly dividends; others, such as many foreign companies, pay every six months. That equation would look like this:

Indicated Dividend = Biannual Dividend per Share × 2

The indicated dividend stays constant until the company formally changes the payout. For example, a company that pays a dividend of 12 cents a share would have an indicated dividend of 48 cents (4 × 12 cents). If the company raises the dividend to 15 cents a share per quarter, the new indicated dividend would be 60 cents (4 × 15 cents).

Figuring out the yield

Yield is the indicated dividend as a percentage of the share price. To calculate yield, you simply divide the indicated dividend by the current share price — what shares in the company are selling for this instant.

Yield = Indicated Dividend ÷ Share Price

Appreciating how pricing affects yield

High yield alone doesn't qualify a dividend stock as a top pick. (Head to the preceding section for more on yield.) You need to know why the yield is high. Two factors affect a stock's yield:

- ✓ **Dividends:** Unless the stock's price also jumps, an increase in dividend payments results in an increase in the stock's yield.

- ✓ **Share price:** Although the indicated dividend remains fairly constant, the share's price changes every day, which means yield changes every day. Small moves in share price lead to tiny changes in yield. However, a large drop in share price (which isn't something shareholders cheer about) gives yield a big boost because the dividend now equals a greater percentage of the share price. A low share price may present a bargain to buy a good yield, or it may be a signal the company is having problems that may lead to a dividend cut.

Tracking yields is a good way to compare companies, especially in the same sector. If Company A pays a 3-percent yield and Company B pays 9 percent, this discrepancy should raise serious questions. Is Company A paying much less than the industry average, or is Company B paying much more? If Company B's yield is out of whack with its competitors, is it because the share price has recently fallen? If the share price has recently fallen and the yield is three times higher, how safe is the dividend?

The price-to-earnings (P/E) ratio

The *price-to-earnings ratio* or *P/E* (sometimes referred to as a *multiple*) indicates how much investors are willing to pay for each dollar of profit they stand to earn per year. For example, if an investor buys a stock with a P/E of 15, he's willing to pay $15 for each dollar of profit, or 15 times the earnings for one share of stock. Another way to look at it is that it will take 15 years to earn back your investment in company profits.

The *P/E ratio* is a good criterion for checking a stock's value relative to the broader market and its competitors. Use the following guidelines to establish your minimum requirement for purchasing a dividend stock:

- ✔ **Below the P/E of the S&P 500 Index:** The rule of thumb is to look for stocks with a P/E below that of the S&P 500 Index, which averages around 18.

- ✔ **Below the industry's average P/E:** If your stock has a high P/E, compare it to the P/Es of its competitors and the industry sector as a whole. If a company's P/E is higher than that of its competitors, the stock is probably overvalued.

- ✔ **Notable exceptions:** Faster growing industries have higher P/Es, so don't automatically discount a stock with a P/E over 18, as it may still be a good value stock. Many of these growth stocks are smaller than the ones on the S&P 500.

A stock with no P/E means the company posted losses. You want to invest in profitable companies to ensure the stability of the dividend payment. Stocks with P/Es higher than 20 mean investors are willing to pay more for $1 of profits because they expect profits to see significant growth. Stocks with P/Es higher than 40 are expected to see very strong growth, but typically that level of P/E means the stock is just overvalued. Stocks with no or excessively high P/Es are speculative buys, not investments.

First things first: Determining earnings per share

Earnings per share, or *EPS* for short, is one of the most important numbers investors use to research companies. Obviously, you want to invest in profitable companies, but is the company that makes a $100 million profit a better buy than a company that makes a profit of just $1 million? Not necessarily. Investors don't care how much the company's total profit is. They want to own the company that gives *them* the most profit, and the best way to gauge that is by looking at profit per share, better known as *earnings per share.*

The easiest way to determine earnings per share is to glance at the company's income statement. It lists two kinds of earnings per share, basic EPS and diluted EPS:

- ✓ **Basic EPS** represents the total shares outstanding, which contains all the stock available to trade at this moment in time.

- ✓ **Diluted EPS** represents total shares outstanding plus other company-issued securities that don't start out as shares of company stock but may eventually turn into shares. These items include

  - **Stock options:** Compensation for managers, which can be turned into stock when it hits a target price.

  - **Warrants:** The rights of certain shareholders to buy new shares prior to public offerings.

  - **Convertible preferred stock:** Preferred shares that can be exchanged for common stock after a predetermined date or price.

  - **Convertible debenture:** Debt instruments that have the potential to turn into common stock.

> Because these securities can change into common shares
> at any time, diluted earnings per share accounts for them
> as part of the total share base. Although these securi-
> ties likely won't all turn into common stock, a significant
> number probably will. Many people prefer to look at
> diluted earnings per share because it provides a worst-
> case scenario of maximum earnings dilution.

Of course, you don't need to worry about calculating earnings per share if the company already reported earnings. You
only need to calculate EPS for the periods not yet reported.
Wall Street stock analysts research the rate of growth in the
company's revenue and earnings, and then make forecasts for
the current quarter or next four quarters. To compare these
predictions to the real results 12 months earlier, analysts
and investors need to reduce these expected future profits to
earnings per shares. You can find future earnings projections
for many companies in Wall Street analyst reports. You use
this formula when you need to calculate your own net profit
projections.

Earnings Per Share = Net Profit ÷ Total Shares Outstanding

Calculating the P/E ratio

Earnings per share alone isn't very useful for measuring a company's relative profitability. An EPS of $50 on shares selling for
$500 is no better than an EPS of 50 cents on shares selling for
$5. The P/E ratio provides a better tool for calculating a stock's
relative value or how much you're paying for that profit.

If you need to calculate a share's P/E ratio, use the following
formula:

P/E ratio = Share price ÷ Annual Earnings per Share

Comparing P/E ratios

The P/E ratio is a great benchmark for comparing any two
companies, particularly if they're in the same sector. If the
P/E ratio for a business sector averages 15, a company with a
P/E of 12 would be undervalued compared to its competitors.
A company with a P/E of 20 would be overvalued. In general,
you want to buy undervalued companies — companies that

are a good value for the profits you're buying. But you need to determine whether the company is undervalued for no good reason or because it's in financial trouble.

The P/E you see in financial newspapers, magazines, and websites is the *Trailing P/E,* or *TTM* (Trailing Twelve Months). The *Forward P/E,* or *Estimated P/E,* is based on earnings projections for the next 12 months. Compare the two numbers. If the Forward P/E is considerably smaller than the Trailing P/E, analysts may be expecting to see the company perform considerably better moving forward. Then again, the analysts may just be overly optimistic.

The price-to-sales ratio

The price-to-sales ratio (PSR) is similar to the P/E discussed in the preceding section, but here you're finding out how much you're paying per dollar of company sales. Instead of earnings per share, you use sales per share:

Sales Per Share = Total Sales ÷ Outstanding Shares

If a company generates sales of $20 million and has three million outstanding shares; its sales per share are $6.67:

$20,000,000 ÷ 3,000,000 = $6.67 Sales Per Share

After calculating sales per share, use the following formula to calculate the PSR:

Price to Sales Ratio (PSR) = Share Price ÷ Sales Per Share

Shares of a company selling for $32 each create a PSR of 4.8:

$32 ÷ $6.67 = 4.8

An undervalued stock has a PSR of 2 or less. A PSR of 1 or less may be a real bargain.

Look for stocks that are undervalued across the board. A stock that's undervalued in one area (such as PSR) but fully valued in another (such as P/E) may mean the company is spending too much in expenses.

The payout ratio

Simply put, the payout ratio tells you how much of the company's profits come back to you as a dividend. You become an investor for the profits, and a dividend investor specifically because you want to pocket some of those profits now. The payout ratio shows you exactly how much of those profits actually land in your pocket.

To calculate the payout ratio, divide the company's dividends per share by the earnings per share (both from the income statement):

Payout Ratio = Dividends per Share ÷ Earnings Per Share

Use the following general guidelines to help measure how well various companies' payout ratios stack up:

- ✔ **Low:** Anything much lower than 50 percent is cause for investigating further. Don't automatically shun companies with low payout ratios because they do have room to grow the size of the dividend. Many growth companies have low payout ratios because they continue to reinvest in the business; these companies offer potential for increased dividend payments as well as capital appreciation in stock price. For example, regional banks often pay out between 30 and 50 percent of their profits. But if a company with a low payout ratio isn't growing fast, you know management can pay out more but chooses not to.

- ✔ **Traditional:** 50 percent is the traditional payout ratio, meaning the company is paying 50 percent of its profits to the shareholders in the form of dividends.

- ✔ **Standard:** 50 to 70 percent is an average range and should not generate any concern. Remember that the range may vary for some industries. Utilities, for example, sometimes pay as high as 80 percent, which is okay for that industry.

- ✔ **High:** A higher payout ratio is always better because it means more money in your pocket. However, you don't want to see a payout ratio of 100 percent or higher. A 100 percent payout ratio means nothing is left to invest in the business. A dividend payout that exceeds the quarterly profit is a big cause for alarm and usually indicates an inevitable dividend cut. Also, a high payout ratio leaves little room for error. If most of the earnings are paid out as dividends, a big drop in earnings one quarter may lead to the company taking on debt to make the payments or an immediate dividend cut. Either way, it's a bad sign.

Master Limited Partnerships may have a payout ratio higher than 100 percent of profits, without the need to take on debt, because of their unusual structure. For more on MLPs, head to Chapter 4.

If a company keeps increasing its dividend but the payout ratio remains below 50 percent, that's a clear sign of strong earnings growth. Procter & Gamble has raised its dividend payment for nearly 60 years while paying out between 40 and 50 percent of its quarterly earnings.

The return on equity

Return on equity (ROE) measures the return on your investment in the company by showing how well the company invested its investors' money and the company's accumulated profits. Return on equity helps you analyze whether the company's management invests its capital well. To calculate ROE, divide net annual profit by total equity:

ROE = Net Annual Profit ÷ Average Annual Shareholder Equity

To determine net annual profit, total the company's net profits presented in each of its four most recent quarterly income statements. To determine equity, average the shareholder equity for those same four quarters; you can find that info on the balance sheets for the most recent quarters.

After you discover the company's ROE, compare it to others in the same sector. The company with the higher ROE is the more profitable one; try to find companies with an ROE of more than 10 percent. A terrible ROE (say, 0 percent) means the company is mismanaged.

When valuing a stock, ask yourself whether the ROE beat the rate of return the company could have earned just by putting the money into Treasury bonds. Look for companies that post an ROE greater than 10. After you've found that, go to the Yahoo! Finance Industry Browser to see whether the company's ROE exceeds others in its sector and if so, how many. You want to buy companies with high ROEs that have seen an upward trend over the past five years.

The quick ratio

One of the best indicators of a company's ability to pay dividends moving forward is the *quick ratio,* which looks to see whether a company has enough liquid assets to cover dividends. A company that has paid a dividend sometime in the past is no better than a one-hit wonder. You have no assurance that the company is likely to pay dividends in the future (as in, after you purchase its stock). The dividend investing strategy seeks to find companies that can afford to pay dividends on a regular basis and increase those dividends over time. These criteria became extremely relevant in the wake of the 2008 and 2009 financial crisis. Many companies with a record of increasing their dividends for decades have cut or eliminated their dividends entirely in order to save cash, so finding a good-looking dividend isn't enough anymore. You need to determine whether the company has the resources to continue the dividend payouts.

Because inventories are the least liquid portion of current assets, the quick ratio removes them from the equation. To derive the quick ratio, subtract inventories from current assets; this removal leaves you with the firm's most liquid assets. Then divide the result by current liabilities. Here's the equation:

Quick Ratio = (Current Assets – Inventories) ÷ Current Liabilities

A quick ratio of 1 indicates that the company holds enough liquid assets to cover all of its current liabilities and is unlikely to cut the dividend. Anything less than 1 means the company's going to have to raid the cookie jar for money to pay its shareholders.

If you want to get extremely conservative, move beyond the quick ratio and just look at the cash on hand. Pure cash provides the best measure of whether a dividend can be paid because the current assets in the quick ratio may include a

lot of accounts receivables from customers who can't pay or aren't required to pay their bills in the time frame that dividends are scheduled to be paid.

The debt covering ratio

Debt isn't necessarily a bad thing, but if a company must continually borrow money just to keep the lights on, that's a sign of trouble. To determine just how manageable a company's debt is, take a look at its *debt covering ratio* to see whether the company generates enough cash from operations to cover current liabilities. To calculate a company's debt covering ratio, plug numbers from its income statement and balance sheet (documents discussed earlier in this chapter) into the following equation:

Debt Covering Ratio = Operating Income ÷ Current Liabilities

The debt covering ratio should equal at least 2. A debt covering ratio below that means the company may not be generating enough to pay both its interest payments and dividends. If this trend continues, the company may soon cut the dividend so it can afford to make its debt payments. You definitely don't want to see a company taking on new debt to pay the dividend.

The debt-to-equity ratio

An additional ratio to check for the stability of the company in general and the dividend in particular is the *debt-to-equity ratio,* which shows how much debt a company has compared to its equity. A high debt-to-equity ratio shows that the company relies on debt rather than equity to finance its operations and presents a clear warning sign. Although debt offers a good way to get financing to grow the company, too much debt can result in large interest payments, leaving less cash for dividend payouts. Also, if the company doesn't earn enough to cover the dividend, it may take on debt to make its payments, creating an unsustainable state for the business. The equation for the debt-to-equity ratio is

Debt-to-Equity Ratio = Total Liabilities ÷ Shareholders' Equity

You can find these numbers on a company's balance sheet. The higher the number, the less stable the company. You want to see a debt-to-equity ratio around 1. Lower is better, but too low means the company may be ignoring growth opportunities to avoid taking on debt.

The price-to-book ratio

The price-to-book ratio (PBR) provides one of the best indications in terms of dollars and cents of whether a company is actually worth what investors are willing to pay for it. *Book value* determines what shareholders would get if they were to liquidate the assets. The shareholder equity, or net worth, is calculated by subtracting liabilities from assets (including intangible assets, such as goodwill). So book value is net worth minus intangible assets. Suppose a company's book value is $500 million and the total value of the outstanding stock is $600 million. If the company were to liquidate its assets, it wouldn't have enough money to buy back its shares from investors, meaning it's overvalued.

Book value = Tangible Assets − Liabilities

To calculate PBR, divide the company's market value or market capitalization (share price times number of shares outstanding) by its book value:

Price-to-Book Ratio (PBR) = Market Value ÷ Book Value

If a company's market value is $12.5 million and the book value is $10 million, the PBR is 125 percent:

$12,500,000 ÷ $10,000,000 = 125 percent

This PBR means the market values the company 25 percent higher than its book value. You want to see PBR equal to or less than 100 percent, indicating the company is undervalued.

Book value can be misleading because the assets category on the balance sheet reflects the company's cost to acquire an asset, not necessarily the asset's current market value. The greater percentage of total assets made up by current assets, the more accurate book value becomes.

Recognizing a Potentially Good Dividend Stock

Just because a company issues a dividend doesn't make it a good dividend stock. It doesn't even make it a good stock to own regardless of the dividend. Many companies pay a dividend in name only. Although the balance sheets, income statements, and cash flow statements I discuss earlier in this chapter provide valuable insight into a company's liquidity and viability at a particular point in time, you need to look at the bigger picture to really determine whether a dividend stock is likely to be a good investment. Specifically, you need to look at how your prospects measure up in relation to six critical criteria (in the following order of importance):

- ✔ Rising dividend payments
- ✔ Fiscal strength
- ✔ Good value
- ✔ Predictable, sustainable cash flow
- ✔ Positive shareholder orientation
- ✔ Good performance in battered industries

The following sections describe these criteria in greater detail and show you how to use them to assess dividend stocks.

Rising dividend payments

Rising dividend payments are the best form of legally obtainable insider information. By announcing to the public that it plans to increase the company's dividend, management tips its hand on what it really thinks about the future of its business. Essentially, the managers proclaim, "We believe we will earn so much more money next year that we can even give a bit more to the shareholders."

However, rising dividend payments may not be good enough. As a savvy investor, consider companies that have a proven track record for consistently raising dividends in good times and bad. Use the following levels of impressiveness as your guide:

- ✔ **Impressive:** Rising dividend payments.

- ✔ **More impressive:** A history of consistently raising dividend payments.

- ✔ **Even more impressive:** A history of consistently raising dividend payments even during bad economic times.

- ✔ **Super impressive:** A history of consistently raising dividend payments in good times and bad, even when the share price is low and yield high.

- ✔ **Super-duper impressive:** The company raising its dividend belongs to the financial services industry, a sector of the market that bore the brunt of the pain and punishment inflicted during the 2008 market crash.

Standard & Poor's created an index called the *S&P 500 Dividend Aristocrats Index* to measures the market performance of a select group of companies that consistently raise their dividends. To get into the index, a company must be a constituent of the S&P 500 index and have increased its dividend every year for at least 25 years. In 2010, 41 constituents were listed in the index, down from 52 in 2009 and 60 in 2008.

Fiscal strength

Obviously, you want to invest in companies that can flex their fiscal muscle, but determining just how fiscally strong a company is can be quite a challenge, particularly if you don't know what to look for. For investors, one of the best indicators of fiscal strength (or lack thereof) is the amount of debt the company has on its books. Although debt is useful in the purchase of capital expenditures, most dividend companies have seen their growth slow, so their debt levels shouldn't be large. A lot of debt can slow earnings growth and may indicate trouble in the company making its dividend payments. A good way to measure a company's debt is through the debt-to-equity ratio.

Good value

You want to buy a stock below its *intrinsic,* or true, value. You want to know what the company expects business to be like for the next 12 to 18 months and what its cash flow will be. After you determine that, you want to apply a multiple to it, such as the P/E ratio, to get a relative value. The P/E ratio is one good way to determine whether a stock is undervalued or overvalued.

Predictable, sustainable cash flow

Strong, sustainable cash flow is perhaps the best sign that a company is healthy. As a dividend investor, you want to put your money in industries, and companies within those industries, that have highly predictable cash flow streams:

- ✓ **Industries:** Banks, railroads, grocery stores, and utilities have a solid reputation for maintaining positive cash flow. Industries with erratic cash flow streams include *cyclical* companies (those more susceptible to the economy's ebbs and flows) and biotechnology firms, which you should avoid.

- ✓ **Companies:** Compare companies within a particular industry to identify the individual companies that perform best in terms of cash flow.

Positive shareholder orientation

A company's shareholder orientation reflects how it treats shareholders — the company's owners. If management appears to be self-serving, maximizing its own pay and bonuses at the expense of the company and its shareholders, be wary. Signs that management places shareholder interests first include the following:

- ✓ **Increasing dividends:** This signal is the best sign of shareholder orientation, because it puts more money in your pocket immediately instead of the company holding onto the cash or investing it in questionable projects.

- ✓ **Paying down debt:** Less debt means greater shareholder equity in the company.

✔ **Share buybacks:** Buybacks remove some of the outstanding shares from the market, boosting share value in two ways. First, with fewer shares, each share represents greater ownership in the company. Second, the rules of supply and demand typically kick in to drive up the share price. To find out about buyback plans, check the company's quarterly filings and press releases. News media often report on buyback plans as well.

✔ **High level of ownership among company insiders:** This marker is the best indication that management's interests align with those of its shareholders. When management owns a lot of stock, it has a vested interest in the company's success. Investigate the number of shares each member of the board of directors owns (and I mean actually owns and not just has the option to buy). A bad sign is when directors have options to buy and don't exercise those options, or only exercise options but don't buy shares on their own. You want to see at least 10 percent insider ownership in smaller companies, although that number may be unreasonable for a big conglomerate.

Good performance in battered industries

When an entire sector gets slammed on Wall Street, good stocks in the same industry tend to fall out of favor at the same time. Look for companies that continue to perform well in pummeled industries such as financial services and real estate.

In these situations, companies with good balance sheets that earn profits and continue to increase their dividends can fly under the radar and sell for bargain prices. In addition, many smaller stocks don't receive much, if any, analytical coverage by the big Wall Street firms. They may not be big or sexy enough for most investors, but you can find some of the best investing opportunities among companies that professional investors ignore.

Chapter 10

Buying and Selling Dividend Stocks

· ·

In This Chapter

▶ Knowing what kind of broker is right for you

▶ Teaming up with a skilled and reputable full-service broker

▶ Going solo by purchasing through a discount broker

▶ Placing various types of buy or sell orders

· ·

*R*egardless of how much you know about investing, you can set up an account with any online discount brokerage and start buying and selling dividend (or any other) stocks this afternoon — assuming, of course, the stock market is open and you can transfer some money into your account.

Before forging ahead with that plan, however, you may want to consider your options. If you're not fully confident in what you're doing or want a professional opinion before you issue a buy or sell order, you may benefit from the expertise of a full-service broker, who doubles as a financial advisor. If you opt to go it alone and process your transactions through a discount broker, you also need to consider the various types of buy and sell orders and how to place orders.

In this chapter, I provide information and guidance to help you choose between teaming up with a full-service broker and flying solo with a discount broker. If you choose the discount broker option, I bring you up to speed on how to issue buy and sell orders on dividend stocks.

The only way you can buy shares yourself is by enrolling in a Direct Purchase Plan (DPP), which I explain in Chapter 6. Otherwise, you must go through a broker — someone who has passed the exams and background check necessary to receive broker certification.

Deciding Between a Full-Service and Discount Broker

In the stock market, you find two species of brokers — full-service and discount:

- ✔ **A full-service broker** does everything a discount broker does and then some. She can help you develop an investment strategy that's suitable for your situation and goals, suggest particular stocks, issue the necessary buy and sell orders on your behalf, and help you make the necessary adjustments to your portfolio as your situation and goals change. Typically, you develop a personal relationship with one stockbroker and/or financial advisor at a brokerage house.

- ✔ **A discount broker** simply follows orders. You tell him to buy 200 shares of XYZ for $20 a share, and that's what he does. If you want to be the master of your own destiny, a discount broker is the choice for you. You do your own research, take full credit for your gains, and take full responsibility for your losses.

Whether you decide to work with a full-service or discount broker, consider costs, minimum balance, products, services, and reputation. Which option is best depends entirely on your preferences. In the following sections, I lay out the pros and cons of each option so that you can make a well-informed choice.

The benefits and drawbacks of a full-service broker

Having an expert around to watch your back and call your attention to potentially incredible investment opportunities may sound like an ideal arrangement, but before you take the plunge, consider the following pros and cons of hiring a full-service broker.

Full-service advantages

A trained, skilled, and experienced full-service broker who's committed to serving your best interests can save you loads of time, energy, and worry while potentially boosting your portfolio's earnings more than enough to cover his fees and commissions. A great broker eats, sleeps, and breathes Wall Street. His job is to research companies, keep his finger on the pulse of the stock market, and earn his clients money, all of which you may not have the time, skill, or interest to do yourself.

Depending on your broker and the relationship you develop, you may receive some additional perks. A good full-service broker examines your financial situation and helps you develop a custom plan. Such a plan is likely to go beyond investing in the stock market and may include developing a budget or savings plan, obtaining sufficient life insurance, offering tax-saving strategies, and planning your estate.

Regardless of whether you fly solo or hire an expert, stay on top of your finances. No one cares as much about your money and how fast it grows as you do. That's because no one else depends on it for their retirement or other goals.

Full-service disadvantages

Enlisting the assistance of an expert always comes with a price tag. In the case of a full-service broker, that price tag may represent a combination of commissions and fees called *transaction costs* and may come in much higher than it would at a discount brokerage. In addition, a good full-service broker may be reluctant to work with investors with small nest eggs and screen them out by requiring higher minimum investments. This bias isn't automatically a bad thing as long as you have the money, but if you don't, it may prevent you from gaining access to some of the most qualified full-service brokers.

Whether you go full-service or discount, focus on keeping costs down. Your total return, or *net profit,* is determined after portfolio costs. If your portfolio earned a profit of $600 one year, but it took $700 worth of expenses to build and maintain it, you actually end up with a $100 loss. To paraphrase Forrest Gump, Wall Street is like a box of chocolates; you never know what you'll get in terms of returns from year to year. So although you can't control how big of a profit you earn, you have complete control over the expenses you pay.

When dealing with full-service brokers, be aware of the possibility of conflicts of interest. If the broker is more concerned with padding her pockets than optimizing your portfolio, she may sell you investment products that are more profitable for her or her investment firm than for you. Brokers have also been known to engage in a shady activity called *churning,* in which they encourage clients to buy and sell more often than necessary so that the brokerage can earn a commission with each transaction.

Always ask your advisor the rationale behind each recommendation. If the advisor can't explain why a particular investment is a good one or you don't like the reason, don't buy the investment. Also keep tabs on the turnover rate of stocks in your portfolio. If your broker is constantly buying and selling (and raking in commissions with each transaction), express your concern and put a stop to it if all the activity isn't clearly in your best interest.

Pros and cons of discount brokers

Discount brokers are best for the do-it-yourselfer. If you like to do your own research, understand how to trade, and don't want investment products pushed on you, you'd probably prefer a discount broker.

The difference between discount brokers and full-service brokers is the same as the difference between a cashier and a top-notch salesperson. Like a cashier, a discount broker simply processes the transaction after you already decided, on your own, what to buy (as opposed to the full-service broker — discussed in the preceding section — who, like a salesperson, helps you choose the right products and services to meet your needs and then processes the transaction). A shady salesperson, however, may try to sell you products and services that put more money in his pocket rather than the products and services that are truly best for you.

Discount broker advantages

When you see the title *discount broker,* you pretty much know the one big advantage that discount brokers have over their full-service counterparts: They charge less to process buy and sell orders. Some charge as little as $3 to process a transaction, regardless of how many shares you buy or sell.

Another big advantage is that except for the relatively small transaction fee, the broker doesn't have any vested interest in what you're buying or selling. Though that may seem like a disadvantage, it prevents any conflict of interest. The broker has nothing to gain through the sale of a particular investment product, so she has no reason to try to influence your choices.

Discount broker disadvantages

With discount brokers, however, you pay less and you get less. You voluntarily give up any expert advice a broker may have to offer. As a result, you're flying solo. However, that doesn't mean you're flying blind. Most discount brokers provide plenty of educational materials and research tools to help you screen for stocks and track market conditions. Some may even provide access to analyst reports from top Wall Street firms.

Another drawback you can expect from some discount brokers is that although the transaction fees are low, the broker may charge other fees to make up the difference, including inactivity fees, fees for closing an account, paperwork fees, IRA custodial fees, and maintenance fees. You can mitigate any losses from these fees by researching brokers carefully, comparing fees, and avoiding brokers who are clearly set up to take their clients to the cleaners.

For details on selecting a discount broker, head to "Finding a Discount Broker" later in this chapter.

Choosing a Full-Service Broker

Many people have neither the interest, ability, nor time to manage their finances. After a hard day's work, most people just want to relax with their friends and family. They don't want to come home to a bunch of homework.

A full-service broker can take the hassles and headaches of dividend investing off your plate. However, a lot of shady characters play the role of full-service broker, so be careful. In the following sections, I show you how to choose a reliable and reputable broker.

Fiduciary and suitability standards

Full-service brokers don't like to be called stockbrokers these days. They prefer more glamorous names such as investment advisor, account executive, financial consultant, financial planner, or retirement specialist. This list can also include analysts, insurance agents, accountants, and attorneys. What the broker calls himself, however, doesn't matter as much as the standard of business he follows: *suitability* or *fiduciary*. The following sections delve into these standards.

Fiduciary

If at all possible, get a full-service broker who follows the fiduciary standard. *Fiduciaries* are responsible for doing the right thing for their clients' investments at all times. The fiduciary is required to work for your best interests and your financial goals first rather than for himself or his firm.

Fiduciaries must also register with the SEC or their state to receive the designation of *Registered Investment Advisor* (RIA). The SEC is in charge of regulating RIAs managing more than $25 million. RIAs with less under management typically register with their states. To determine whether a particular firm is an RIA, perform a search at www.adviserinfo.sec.gov.

Fiduciaries typically pursue further studies to receive advanced accreditation, such as the following:

- ✔ Certified Financial Planner (CFP)
- ✔ Chartered Financial Analyst (CFA)
- ✔ Chartered Financial Consultant (ChFC)
- ✔ Certified Public Accountant/Personal Financial Specialist (CPA/PFS)

Neither the federal nor any state government requires a person to hold any of these designations or have any kind of degree in order to work as a "financial planner." If your advisor is a registered investment advisor (RIA), a CPA, or an attorney, you can be sure they're acting as a fiduciary. If you see CFP, CFA, or ChFC after an advisor's name, that person has been professionally certified to have met certain education and ethical requirements, but none of these designations guarantees the person is a fiduciary. Always ask.

Suitability

Most stockbrokers follow the suitability standard — the less rigorous of the two. Unlike fiduciary, *suitability* essentially says the broker doesn't have to put your interests first. As long as the product is suitable to your goals and risk tolerance, the broker isn't required to sell the best or cheapest product. He can sell you the product that pays him the highest commissions and fees.

For example, although many mutual funds track the S&P 500 Index, your broker can stick you with a fund that charges an expense ratio of 1 percent and pays him a front load of 5 percent instead of putting you in a comparable no-load fund with an expense ratio of 0.18 percent.

Stockbrokers who follow the suitability model only need to register with the National Association of Securities Dealers, a nongovernmental industry regulating body.

Investment preferences

Like individual investors, brokers have preferences in terms of strategy. Some brokers prefer high-growth stocks, and others focus more on value. Some tend to prefer mutual funds over investing in individual stocks. Though you want someone who knows all the available investment vehicles, you also want someone who's as committed as you are to dividend investing. If the broker is more bullish on growth stocks, his focus may wander from the types of companies you're interested in investing in.

Before hiring a broker, ask a few questions about the strategy he recommends without letting him know your preferences. Ask what percentage of your portfolio he would recommend investing in growth stocks, dividend stocks, and bonds. Ask whether growth or dividend stocks are a better choice right now. Ask about the tradeoffs between growth and dividend investing. The answers the broker provides should paint a pretty good picture of his preferences.

Fee structure

No financial advisor works for free. They all have some way of receiving compensation for their services. This compensation typically comes in one of the following forms:

- ✔ **Fee-only compensation:** The financial advisor charges a fee for her advice and for managing your portfolio. The fee is usually an hourly rate, flat fee, retainer, or a percentage of the profits your portfolio earns. Paying a percentage of your profits is usually best because it minimizes potential conflicts of interest and aligns your advisor's interests with yours. If your portfolio gains, she makes more money. If it declines, she makes less (or no) money.

- ✔ **Fee-based compensation:** The financial advisor can charge fees and collect commissions from any third-party products she sells. The idea here is that the commissions can offset some of the costs you're required to pay. The commissions, however, have the potential of creating a conflict of interest.

- ✔ **Commissions:** Brokers compensated with commissions are mainly salespeople working for commissions rather than for their clients. Even well-intentioned advisors are likely to be swayed into selling products that put more money in their pockets.

In Chapters 6 and 8, I recommend implementing a dollar cost averaging approach to diminish risk. And throughout the book I recommend a dividend reinvestment strategy. Each of these strategies requires investing relatively small amounts of money over time. Some full-service brokers may let you reinvest your dividends with no additional fee, but some don't. When shopping for a full-service broker, ask about the cost of implementing these strategies. Small fees can add up quickly when they're charged to you on a monthly or even a quarterly basis.

Ask your financial advisor how she gets paid and whether she's getting paid to make certain recommendations. Don't be afraid. It's your money, and you're the client. You wouldn't buy a car without asking the price, so why would you buy stock without asking? Consider it comparison shopping. Ask whether you can get something similar for less. Get a few quotes. You may be able to negotiate a lower fee. Tell the financial advisor you want a signed document outlining her fee structure and fiduciary status before becoming a client.

While you're asking about the cost, ask about how risky the investment is as well. Sometimes the upside isn't worth the risk of losing money.

Conducting your own background check

When you're in the market for a financial advisor or full-service broker, ask friends, family members, and colleagues for recommendations. Choosing someone who's provided satisfactory service to at least one person you know is usually a good place to start. You can then do your own research to double-check the person's or the firm's credentials. Or, if you still have no leads, you can start poking around online to find some promising candidates.

To find reputable full-service brokers or investment advisors, check out the following sources:

- ✔ National Association of Personal Financial Advisors (NAPFA) is an organization of fee-only financial planners. NAPFA members agree to follow certain standards and must achieve a certain level of competence. Visit www. napfa.org.

- ✔ Barron's http://online.barrons.com publishes an annual survey of discount and full-service brokers.

- ✔ Financial Industry Regulatory Authority (FINRA) at www. finra.org provides free broker reports. Each report lists any complaints or penalties filed against the broker or his firm.

Finding a Discount Broker

If you want to make your own investment decisions and don't need the premium services offered by a full-service broker, you may prefer to use a discount broker. Most of them allow you to trade online for a very low commission.

First, decide on your main criteria for a discount broker. Is it the cheapest trade, the best trading system, the best research tools and information, or something else? After deciding what's most important, head online and comparison shop. Following is a list of the top discount brokers in alphabetical order. All have solid reputations, but I'm not recommending one over any other:

- ✔ Charles Schwab: www.schwab.com or 866-855-9102

- ✔ E*Trade: https://us.etrade.com or 800-387-2331

- ✔ Fidelity: www.fidelity.com or 800-Fidelity

- ✔ Firstrade: www.firstrade.com or 800-869-8800

- ✔ Interactive Brokers: www.interactivebrokers.com or 877-442-2757

- ✔ Muriel Siebert: www.siebertnet.com or 800-872-0444

- ✔ Options Xpress: www.optionsxpress.com or 888-280-8020

- ✔ Scottrade: www.scottrade.com or 800-619-7283

- ✔ SogoTrade: www.sogotrade.com or 888-709-SOGO

- ✔ TD Ameritrade: www.tdameritrade.com or 800-454-9272

- ✔ TradeKing: www.tradeking.com or 877-495-5464

- ✔ Vanguard: www.vanguard.com or 877-662-7447

- ✔ Wells Fargo: www.wellsfargo.com or 800-869-3557

When comparing discount brokers, consider the cost of implementing a dollar cost averaging strategy and dividend reinvestment strategy with each broker. Some online brokers offer automatic investing with lower commissions and fees per trade, which is perfect for a dollar cost averaging strategy. If you plan on reinvesting dividends, you also want to make sure that your reinvestment transactions are free or at least reasonable. (To determine what's "reasonable," comparison shop.)

Buying and Selling Shares

Everyone knows you can buy and sell shares of stock on the stock market. Some investors, however, don't realize the nuances of the different buy and sell orders: market orders, time orders, limit orders, stop-loss orders, and so on. By understanding these different types of orders and using them correctly, you can maximize your dividend profits and minimize your potential losses. This knowledge is especially helpful if you're working with a discount broker, who doesn't provide the same guidance as a full-service broker.

Market orders

The *market order* is the simplest, most straightforward way to buy or sell stock. You place an order to buy or sell shares, and it gets filled as quickly as possible at the best possible price. Market orders carry no time or price limitations. Stocks with high trading volume process the trade immediately. Stocks with a low trading volume may take longer to trade and experience a wide *bid-ask spread* — the difference between the seller's asking price and the buyer's bid amount.

Market orders are the only trades that always go through on the day they're placed. The downside of the market order is you never know what price you've paid until after the trade is completed. If the market is very volatile on the day you place the order, you can end up paying a price very different from the one you were expecting.

Limit orders

Limit orders are the flip side of market orders. With a market order, you want the trade to go through immediately and aren't price sensitive. With a *limit order,* you want a specific price for a purchase or sale regardless of how long getting that price takes. You're willing to wait to get what you want.

Just remember that you may wait forever if the stock never reaches your limit. Limit orders also allow you to trade without having to pay close attention to the market.

Say you want to buy shares of Carrel Industries. You've done your homework and think that the price is currently overvalued at $25. You can put in a limit order for 100 shares at $20. If the share price drops to that threshold, you get the stock at your price. Otherwise, your order remains unfilled.

You can also use a limit order on the sell side. If you bought shares at $20 and the stock is moving higher, you can put a limit order in to sell the shares at $25.

Limit orders (among other kinds of trades) often don't go through on the day you place them, so you need to place a time order (which I explain in the following section) with a limit order.

Time orders

Two kinds of *time orders* determine how long an order (such as a limit order) remains in effect:

- ✔ **Day orders:** *Day orders* expire at the end of the trading day on which you place them. If the stock you want is at $42 and you place a day order to buy shares at $40, the order expires unfilled if the stock doesn't fall to $40 during the trading session.

- ✔ **Good-till-canceled:** Just like it sounds, the *good-till-canceled order* stays in effect until one of two things happen: Either the stock hits the price you want and the trade goes through, or you call your broker and actively cancel the order (although note that some brokers put a 30 or 60 day limit on good-till-canceled orders).

Stop-loss orders

Stop-loss orders work similarly to limit orders but with a different strategy. With a limit order, you know how much profit you want to earn, so you place a limit to sell your shares at the specific price that locks in that profit. With the stop-loss order, your stock is rising and you want to let it ride to see how far the stock goes while protecting the capital gains already in the share price if the shares fall.

The stop-loss order puts in a sell order to sell your shares if they fall to a specific price below where the shares are today, usually 10 percent below the current share price. For instance, if you bought Carrel Industries at $20 and it's now trading at $30, you put the stop-loss order in at $27. If the stock falls to $27, your shares are sold. That order gives the dividend stock enough room to bounce around in a day-to-day trading range yet protects 70 percent of your profit.

Trailing stop orders

Trailing stops are a technique that uses stop-loss orders to preserve your dividend stock's profits. *Trailing stops* are stop-loss orders that trail the movement of the stock's price. As the stock moves higher, you keep moving the stop-loss order higher to protect more profits.

In the preceding section's example, shares of Carrel Industries are selling for $30 and you have a stop-loss at $27, or a 10-percent drop in price. If the stock rises to $36, you move the stop-loss order to $32.40 to maintain that 10-percent floor. If the stock moves to $40, you cancel that stop-loss and replace it with a new one at $36. By trailing the stock by the same amount as the price increases, the stop-loss progressively protects more and more of your profits than if you had left it at $27.

Brokers rarely institute trailing stops, so you can't just set it and forget it. You have to actively manage your trailing stops.

Short sales

Wall Street calls buyers *long on stocks.* You expect your stock to move higher, and you have unlimited profit potential. However, you can also profit from a falling market or declines in individual stocks. Selling a stock first with the expectation of buying it back later at a lower price is known as *selling short* or *shorting a stock*. This strategy is one of the main ways to make money in a bear market. Instead of buying low and selling high, you first sell high with the hope of later buying low.

Selling short is a three-step process.

1. You borrow shares.

Your broker borrows the shares you want to sell from either his own inventory or one of his clients. If the broker doesn't have easy access, he may need to go into the market to buy the shares for you to borrow.

2. You sell the shares.

You tell your broker to sell the shares with either a market order or a limit order. Then your account is credited with the proceeds from the sale.

3. You buy new shares and return them to the lender.

To close the trade, you buy shares and give them back to the client or broker you borrowed them from. If the system works in your favor, the stock falls and you buy the shares at a lower price than you sold them for, garnering a profit for yourself (because you paid less than you received for them). If you sell 100 shares at $30 and buy them back at $20, you earn $1,000 (100 shares times $10).

You can put a stop-loss order on a short sale too, to limit the potential losses.

Chapter 11

Staying Current on Tax Laws

. . . .

In This Chapter

▶ Knowing how Uncle Sam taxes dividends

▶ Differentiating between qualifying and nonqualifying dividends

▶ Unraveling the complexities of taxing dividends in mutual funds

▶ Grasping the dividend tax ramifications from ETFs, MLPs, and REITs

▶ Staying on top of changes in the tax code

. . . .

*S*uccessful investing isn't only about earning handsome
returns but also about how much of that money you walk
away with at the end. If your investment earns an 8 percent
return that's taxed at 30 percent, your net return is actually
only 5.6 percent (.08 return × .7 untaxed percentage = .056
after-tax return). Instead of earning $80 on a $1,000 investment,
you pocket only $56. Tax that same investment at only 15 per-
cent, and your net return climbs to 6.8 percent (.08 return × .85
untaxed percentage = .068 after-tax return). Instead of netting
only $56 per $1,000 invested, you keep $68.

If you're reinvesting your returns, taxes take an even bigger
bite out of your net profit, because each dollar the taxman
takes is one fewer dollar you can put back into the stock
market. As a result, your compounding dividends compound
less dramatically.

To maximize your net return on investments, brush up on and
stay current with the tax code. This chapter highlights key
areas of interest to dividend investors and shows you how to
keep up with changes in how the government taxes earnings.

Consult a tax specialist for specific advice. Although this chapter provides plenty of valuable information on how to lighten the tax burden on your investment returns, I'm not a tax specialist. Plus, tax laws do change. The information in this chapter is intended to help you gain a better understanding of investment-related tax issues and identify tax issues you may want to discuss with your accountant when developing your investment strategy.

Dividend Taxation

The government often uses tax policy to encourage certain economic and consumer activity. After the tech bubble burst in 2000, for example, the economy slowed. To pull the country out of another recession, in 2003 President George W. Bush signed into law the Jobs and Growth Tax Relief Reconciliation Act (JGTRRA), which cut taxes on ordinary income, capital gains, *and* dividends.

Dividends are taxed in the year they're received. The time the payment arrives, not the *date of declaration* (date the board of directors announces the dividend payment), determines when the dividend is taxed. Head to Chapter 2 for more on the date of declaration and other important dividend-related dates.

The drawbacks of double taxation

In taxing dividends, the government engages in a form of double dipping, more commonly referred to as *double taxation*. With double taxation, the government collects taxes on the same money twice: It taxes the company's profits (typically at a rate of 35 percent) and then taxes the dividends investors receive, which come out of the company's after-tax profits. Prior to JGTRRA, this arrangement meant the government could receive 35 percent of a company's profits and then up to another 38.6 percent of each investor's cut!

Double taxation has several effects on how companies do business and where investors choose to put their money:

> ✔ To dodge the double-taxation bullet, many corporations choose to invest all of their profits in research, development, and other ventures rather than distribute a portion of the profits to investors.

✔ Investors also are motivated to dodge the double-taxation bullet by investing in companies that *don't* pay dividends. Instead of relying on dividends for their returns, investors tend to shift their focus to growth and rely on share price appreciation for their returns when they sell their stock.

✔ The threat of double taxation may drive management to invest in projects with less potential merely to avoid the double tax, which may be bad for the company and investors.

The JGTRRA tax break

If dividends meet certain qualifications the JGTRRA reduced the dividend tax rate from the investor's ordinary income tax rate to a maximum of 15 percent for most taxpayers or 5 percent for taxpayers in the 10- to 15-percent tax brackets. This tax cut represented a huge savings for dividend investors, as shown in Table 11-1, which compares the old and new rates, their pieces of your dividend per $1,000, and how much the new rates save you.

Table 11-1   JGTRRA's Effect on Dividend Tax Rates

Old Tax Rate/ Bracket	New Tax Rate	Old Tax	New Tax	Savings
10%	5%	$100	$50	$50
15%	5%	$150	$50	$100
27%	15%	$270	$150	$120
30%	15%	$300	$150	$150
35%	15%	$350	$150	$200
38.6%	15%	$386	$150	$236

These new, lower tax rates triggered three major changes in the market:

✔ **They leveled the playing field for growth and income investors.** Prior to this act, growth stocks were more attractive from a tax perspective because capital gains were taxed at a significantly lower rate than dividends.

✓ **The tax cuts put more money in taxpayers' pockets, fueling the economy.** Dividend-paying companies could afford to pay higher dividends, and as demand for stock rose, so did share prices.

✓ **More companies started paying dividends.** Reduction of the long-term capital gains tax in the early 1980s triggered a trend of decreasing dividend payments. To avoid high taxes on dividends, more companies invested more of their profits in growth, and investors preferred reaping their rewards in capital gains, which were taxed at a lower rate. The JGTRRA reversed this trend.

Finding qualifying dividends

All dividends aren't created equal. Some qualify for JGTRRA tax breaks, and some don't. Almost all dividends paid by U.S. corporations qualify for the lower tax rate. Notable exceptions included REITs (real estate investment trusts, covered in Chapter 5) and master limited partnerships (MLP, which I discuss in Chapter 4). If the dividends qualify for the lower tax rate, the investor needs to meet the holding period requirements I spell out in the following section. Dividends paid by foreign corporations may qualify if the corporation's stock or American Depository Receipts (ADRs) are traded on well-established U.S. securities markets or the corporation is eligible under a tax treaty with the United States.

Determining which stocks don't qualify is a little easier than determining which stocks do qualify. Any item in the following list can *disqualify* a dividend from preferred tax treatment under the JGTRRA:

✓ Dividends from preferred stock that's treated more as an interest-bearing debt instrument than a true dividend-paying stock.

✓ Dividends paid into tax-deferred retirement accounts, including IRAs, 401(k) plans, and deferred annuities. Tax is levied as ordinary income when you withdraw money.

✓ Dividends from money market accounts.

✓ Dividends from insurance policies.

✓ Dividends from mutual funds attributable to interest and short-term capital gains.

- Majority of dividends from S-Corporations.

- Dividends paid to investors named as nominees.

- Dividends paid by tax-exempt organizations, including some mutual savings banks and savings institutions such as credit unions, mutual insurance companies, farmers' cooperatives, nonprofit voluntary employee benefit associations (VEBAs), and building and loan associations.

- Stocks, including MLPs and REITs, that have built-in tax preferences. See "MLP and REIT Taxation" later in this chapter for details.

Meeting the holding-period requirement

Even if the dividends come from a qualified company, another factor that can disqualify dividends from the JGTRRA-preferred taxed rate is a failure on your part to hold the shares long enough. You can't just buy a dividend stock a day before the *ex-dividend date* (point after which the dividend is removed from the share price), sell your shares the day after you collect the next dividend, and expect to receive preferential tax treatment under the JGTRRA. You have to hold your shares for a reasonable amount of time. What's reasonable? That depends on whether you're holding common or preferred stock:

- **Common stock:** You must hold your shares for more than 60 days during the 121-day period beginning 60 days prior to the ex-dividend date. That is, you have to buy your shares at least one day (up to 60 days) before the ex-dividend date and then hold them for at least 61 days.

- **Preferred stock:** You must hold your shares for more than 90 days during the 181-day period beginning 90 days prior to the ex-dividend date. That is, you have to buy your shares at least one day (up to 90 days) before the ex-dividend date and then hold them for at least 91 days.

The day you purchase your shares doesn't count, but the day you sell your shares does. Chapter 2 gives you more info on common and preferred stock.

When the company issues you a federal tax form 1099-DIV, it lists the monetary value of the dividends that potentially qualify for the lower tax rate. Whether they do qualify depends on how long you held the shares. It's up to you to determine whether they qualify or not. Check the ex-dividend date and the date you bought and sold the shares to determine whether your dividends qualify for the lower tax rate. Better yet, check the ex-dividend date and your purchase date prior to selling shares and make sure you've met the holding requirement *before* you sell.

Keeping up with changing tax rates

In the ten years following the passage of the JGTRRA, the taxation of dividends saw some changes. At the time this book was published, the most recent rates came from the American Taxpayer Relief Act of 2012. These rates are in Table 11-2. As always, consult an accountant for any changes in tax rates.

Table 11-2   Dividend Tax Rates as of 2012 Tax Law

Ordinary Income Tax Rate	Ordinary Dividend Tax Rate	Qualified Dividend Tax Rate
10%	10%	0%
15%	15%	0%
25%	25%	15%
28%	28%	15%
33%	33%	15%
35%	35%	15%
39.5%	39.5%	20%

The Patient Protection and Affordable Care Act, better known as Obamacare, created a new Net Investment Income Tax (NIIT) of 3.8% that became effective in 2013. This tax applies to dividends, capital gains, and other forms of passive investment income if you're married with a modified adjusted gross income of more than $250,000 or single with a modified adjusted gross income of more than $200,000. Unlike the thresholds for ordinary income tax rates and the qualified dividend rates, the NIIT threshold is not inflation-adjusted.

Delaying taxes with tax-deferred accounts

If you're holding your dividend stocks in an IRA, KEOGH, SEP, or other tax-deferred retirement account, you can forget all this business about holding-period requirements. Any dividends you receive are added to the pot tax-free (for now, anyway). You pay taxes only when you withdraw money.

Being able to reinvest tax-free for decades provides a great benefit, in that you have more money to invest. With tax-deferred accounts, you reinvest 100 percent of your income. The big trade-off for being allowed to reinvest your dividends and grow your capital gains for years without paying taxes is that you may not receive the lower tax rate. When you begin withdrawing your money, it may be taxed at the same rate as ordinary income.

Most tax-deferred accounts are prohibited from owning master limited partnerships. The tax accounting on these companies is too complicated to handle in a tax-deferred fund.

The Tax on Dividends from Mutual Funds

Mutual funds are pass-through investment vehicles: If the funds pass at least 90 percent of the portfolio's profits to the shareholders, the fund's tax obligation gets passed through to the shareholders as well. If the fund holds any income, it must pay taxes on that, so most funds pass through 100 percent of their profits. The profits that mutual funds distribute can take many forms, each with its own tax rules:

- ✔ **Capital gains:** From the sale of assets
- ✔ **Ordinary dividends:** Mostly from stocks, but can include all kinds of taxable income
- ✔ **Interest distributions exempt from taxation:** Such as municipal bonds or other obligations from state and local governments

✔ **Interest:** From bonds and other debt obligations

✔ **Non-dividend distributions:** A portion of your initial investment returned to you, which isn't considered income

To further complicate the determination of tax rates on profits is the fact that holding requirements for lower tax rates apply to both how long the fund holds certain stocks and how long you hold your shares in the fund. At the end of the tax year, your mutual fund issues you a 1099-DIV indicating which dividends and capital gains qualify for the lower tax rates and which don't *inside the fund.* To determine whether these dividends and capital gains actually qualify for you, you must account for the length of time you held your shares in the fund. In the following sections, I explain how these two levels of criteria contribute in determining the tax rates for profits on dividend stocks held in a mutual fund.

Don't assume because the fund says this amount of dividends are qualified that they actually receive the lower tax rate. The fund doesn't take into consideration *your* holding period when it declares qualified dividends. It just lets you know that the fund has done its part to make them "potentially" qualified by holding them for the 61-day period. Both you and the fund need to hold the appropriate shares for 61 days of the 121-day period surrounding the ex-dividend date. But they don't have to be the exact same 61 days.

Your 1099-DIV

Each year, typically in January or February, but sometimes as late as early April, you can expect to receive a late Christmas present from each of your dividend stocks and mutual funds: a 1099-DIV. The 1099-DIV reports all your taxable income distributions from the fund so you can account for them appropriately on your tax return. If your present doesn't arrive, contact the fund company for the information.

The following sections describe the contents of certain elements of this form so that you can gain a clearer understanding of how these amounts are taxed.

Box 1a. Total ordinary dividends

The amount in this box represents all dividends (both qualified and unqualified) paid by the fund.

Box 1b. Qualified dividends

If your mutual fund owns stock in companies that pay qualified dividends, a portion or all of the total ordinary dividends
reported in box 1a may appear in box 1b, depending on how
long the fund held its shares. Remember that these figures
represent the dividends that qualify for the mutual fund. To
determine whether they qualify for you, head to the earlier
section "Meeting the holding-period requirement."

Box 2a. Total capital gain distribution

Box 2a is guilty of a misnomer. Instead of being called "total
capital gain distribution," it should be labeled "total long-term
capital gain distribution" because the fund's short-term capital gains are reported as unqualified dividends.

Capital gains inside mutual funds are just like capital gains in
individual stocks. If a fund sells a stock for more than it paid
for its shares, the profit is a capital gain. If the fund held the
sold asset for more than one year, the profit is treated as a
long-term capital gain.

Even though you haven't cashed out your fund shares and
regardless of whether those long-term capital gains were
reinvested or distributed to shareholders, you need to pay
taxes on them.

Don't get stuck paying taxes on gains you never received.
Mutual funds may earn capital gains throughout the year, but
they distribute their long-term capital gains only at the end
of the year. Although this setup may seem like a positive to
the guy who buys late in the year, it's not. Any capital gain
distribution lowers the mutual fund's net asset value (NAV). If
you buy near the end of the year and receive the distribution,
but the fund's share price drops, you end up even. However,
you may still get stuck paying taxes on these gains that left
you cash neutral. Before buying a mutual fund late in the year,
check its capital gains distribution date.

Other important dividend taxation considerations

Although the 1099-DIV does some computing for you (see the
preceding section), it doesn't give you everything you need
to know. The following sections point out a couple of other

numbers to be aware of as well as a situation that may affect your dividends' taxation.

Nonqualified dividends

Nonqualified dividends are all dividends paid to the fund that fail to qualify for the lower tax rates, as I describe in "Finding qualifying dividends" earlier in this chapter. For these dividends, you pay taxes at your rate for ordinary income. Surprisingly, the 1099-DIV doesn't include a box for this number. You have to figure it out yourself:

Total Ordinary Dividends – Qualified Dividends = Nonqualified Dividends

For example, if the fund reports $280 in total ordinary dividends and $200 in qualified dividends, it earned $80 in nonqualified dividends:

$280 – $200 = $80

Because the fund reports everything that's not a capital gain as a dividend, nonqualified dividends may not actually be dividends. The mutual fund reports income that falls into any or all of the following distribution categories as nonqualified dividends:

- ✔ **Nonqualified dividends:** These are dividends from stocks not held long enough to qualify for the lower tax rate. If it's a nonqualified dividend for the fund, it's not qualified for you.

- ✔ **Taxable interest:** Any interest the fund earned from Treasury bills or other debt in which the fund held cash is taxable interest.

- ✔ **Short-term capital gains:** Profits on assets held for less than a year are short-term capital gains, paid to fund shareholders as dividends.

Short-term capital gains you receive from the fund refer to how long the fund held the stock in the portfolio, not how long you held the fund shares.

Because short-term capital gain distributions are taxed at the shareholder's maximum tax rate along with nonqualified dividends, treating short-term capital gains as taxable income may seem harmless, but it's not. For instance, if you earn a short-term capital gain in any other (non-mutual fund) invest-ment you sell and suffer any kind of capital loss in a separate investment, you can use the loss to offset the tax liability on the gain. However, because short-term capital gain distribu-tions aren't broken out in mutual funds, you have to pay taxes on them at the full rate no matter what. Even if the fund lists the short-term capital gains on the 1099-DIV, they're still con-sidered ordinary, nonqualified dividends. You can't lower the tax liability with a capital loss.

Reinvested dividends

When mutual funds reinvest dividends, additional tax issues arise:

- ✓ Even though the fund reinvests the dividends, you must pay taxes on them, just as if you had received a cash distribution.

- ✓ The new shares have their own cost basis, different from your initial investment. The *cost basis* is the price used to determine capital gains or losses. Typically, it's the price paid for an asset, but not always. Keep track of the cost basis of these new shares bought with dividends because when you sell these shares, you use that number to cal-culate your capital gain or loss on the sale.

- ✓ The new shares have a new purchase date. Keep track of this date to determine whether any distributions or capi-tal gains related to these shares meet the holding period requirements for lower tax rates.

Your holding period for capital gains

Just like a stock, you earn a capital gain if you sell your fund shares for more than you paid. If you sell for less than you paid you get a capital loss. If you held your fund shares for more than a year, you pay the lower long-term capital gains rate. Less than a year, and you pay your ordinary tax rate.

January dividends

If the fund receives dividends in the last quarter of the year but distributes the dividend in January, the fund can treat the distribution as if it were paid on December 31 the prior year. It may look like a mistake, but it's not. This situation means these dividends also get taxed as part of the prior year's income. Tax rates again depend on the holding period; I dis-cuss holding period requirements earlier in the chapter.

A tax break of sorts

Although mutual funds contain some tax "penalties," such as not allowing you to offset short-term capital gains in mutual funds with short-term capital losses in other investments, they do provide a backhanded tax break. Mutual funds lower taxable income by using the portfolio's earnings to pay off the fund's expense ratio. For example, if the fund yields a dividend 3 percent of fund assets but the expense ratio is 1 percent of fund assets, it uses the first 1 percent of income to pay all the management costs, leaving the investor with a net yield of 2 percent.

Although you end up with less cash in your pocket, this strategy lessens your dividend tax liability and keeps the fund from having to sell assets to cover expenses, which would incur additional costs.

The Tax on Dividends from ETFs

Like mutual funds, EFTs (exchange traded funds) are investment companies and share many of the same traits. Dividend-related tax issues are similar between the two as well. When investing in dividend-focused ETFs, keep the following tax issues in mind:

- ✔ ETFs must distribute all dividends to their shareholders.

- ✔ ETFs must hold stocks that pay qualified dividends the required 61-day holding period to receive the preferred tax rate.

- ✔ To receive qualified dividends from an ETF, hold the ETF shares in your personal account for the required holding period as well.

- ✔ Interest, short-term capital gains, and nonqualified dividends are taxed as ordinary income.

- ✔ Most ETFs don't pay long-term capital gains. Some do, but it's very rare. If yours does, go to the ETF company's website or give the company a call to see what it says about long-term capital gains.

ETFs can hold many kinds of assets, each with exotic tax structures. If you're investing for dividends, be sure your ETF holds equities. Consult a tax professional for specific advice related to your investments.

MLP and REIT Taxation

Some of the most attractive dividend stocks play by entirely different tax rules than those that apply to the majority of dividends. In the following sections, I describe the unique tax advantages (and some drawbacks) of real estate investment trusts (REITs, Chapter 5) and master limited partnerships (MLPs, Chapter 4).

REIT taxation

Real estate investment trusts (REITs) are similar to mutual funds. They allow investors to share in profits from a pool of real estate investments without having to actually purchase individual properties. When the real estate market is cruising along, REITs generally perform very well as dividend stocks, delivering yields of between 6 and 9 percent. In addition, the dividends usually keep flowing even when share prices take a dip because to preserve their tax advantages, they must pay out at least 90 percent of their income to shareholders in the form of dividends.

By agreeing to pay out nearly all their income and only invest in certain types or real estate assets, the tax code gives REITs a unique advantage over other dividend-paying corporations. REITs avoid paying any corporate taxes and pass through the tax obligation to their shareholders. At the end of the year, shareholders receive a Form 1099, which reports cash distributions in three forms: dividends, long-term capital gains, and return on capital.

Dividends for REITs

Unfortunately for investors, these dividends don't qualify for preferential treatment under JGTRRA. They're taxed as ordinary income. (The section "Dividend Taxation" earlier in the chapter gives you more information on how the JGTRRA legislation changed dividend taxation.)

Long-term capital gains for REITs

Capital gains can be included in your dividend payment. If the REIT sold assets at a profit and they qualify as long-term capital gains, you pay the lower tax rate on this portion of the dividends.

Return on capital for REITs

REIT dividends also contain a component called *return on capital* — the portion of a REIT's dividend over and above its taxable income, primarily due to depreciation of assets. In essence, the firm returns some of your investment to you based on the fact that the value of the real estate holdings depreciates over time. Although this move puts some tax-deferred cash in your pocket now, it lowers the cost basis of your shares, increasing the capital gains you must report when you sell your shares:

Initial Investment – Return on Capital = New Cost Basis

Return on capital isn't taxed, at least not when you pocket the money. The tax liability is deferred until you sell your shares in the REIT.

Suppose you buy 100 shares of a REIT at $50 a share, for a total of $5,000. The company pays a 9-percent yield of $450. Of that, $150 qualifies as ordinary dividends, and $300 is a return of capital. Even though you paid $5,000 for your shares, the IRS now lists your cost basis as $4,700:

$5,000 – $300 = $4,700

A year later you sell the shares for $60 each, or $6,000 for a profit of $1,000 (not counting the $300 you received in return on capital):

$6,000 – $1,000 = $5,000

With the long-term capital gains rate of 15 percent, you may expect to pay $150 in taxes:

$1,000 × 0.15 = $150

However, the return on capital lowered your cost basis to $4,700, so you have to report capital gains of $1,300:

$6,000 – $4,700 = $1,300

You tax bill rises to $195 rather than the $150 on your original cost basis:

$1,300 × 0.15 = $195

The one shining light here is that you pay the 15-percent tax rate rather than the higher rate for ordinary dividends.

REITs may require you to pay a bigger chunk of the tax bill, but don't let that scare you off. The important number to look at is your return *after taxes*. You may walk away with more money in your pocket by investing in a REIT with a 7-percent yield, even after paying taxes, than you would by investing in a non-REIT with a 2- or 3-percent yield.

MLP taxation

Master Limited Partnerships (MLPs; see Chapter 4) dodge the double-taxation bullet because they aren't corporations. They're true partnerships in which every investor is a partner. Investors aren't even called shareholders (they're *unitholders*), and partnerships don't pay taxes. The profits and expenses are divided proportionally among the partners. Profits pass tax-free through the partnership to the unitholders, who must report their profits on their individual tax returns. Unfortunately for investors, this arrangement can severely complicate tax calculations and significantly add to the paperwork.

Before investing in an MLP, consult a tax specialist and get answers to the following questions (I discuss these issues in more detail later in this section):

- In how many different states does the MLP do business?

- How many units can I purchase in a specific MLP before I have to file a tax return in each state in which the partnership does business?

Unlike REITs and mutual funds, MLPs don't have to pay a cash distribution to investors. You can owe tax on MLP earnings without actually receiving any cash. However, most MLPs have internal governing agreements that require them to pay out all their available cash flow.

Rather than a 1099-DIV, the MLP issues a Schedule K-1 with your cash distributions broken out into various sources of income, each of which may be taxed at a different rate, as explained in the following sections.

Dividends for MLPs

Like the REIT, the MLP's taxable income in the form of dividends is taxed at your ordinary income tax rate. It isn't eligible for the preferred lower tax rate. Flip to "Dividend Taxation" earlier in the chapter for more on the varying tax rates for investment income.

Long-term capital gains for MLPs

Capital gains can be included in your dividend payment and are taxed at the preferred rate.

State taxes

You also have to pay taxes to each state the MLP does business in, which can be a paperwork nightmare. Your tax adviser can help you figure out which forms you need to fill out for whom.

Return on capital for MLPs

All cash distributions that don't fall under taxable income are considered a return on capital. This recapture of depreciation isn't taxed now, but it lowers the taxable cost basis of your shares. When you sell your shares later, only the part that represents a true capital gain from your initial cost basis is eligible for the lower capital gains tax rate. All the return on capital that lowered your tax basis is taxed at the rate of your ordinary income.

The taxable cost basis continues to fall as long as you hold the MLP, so, the longer you hold the shares, the more tax you pay when you sell.

Most tax computer programs tell you where to input the numbers. However, with MLPs, you're usually better off hiring a tax professional.

Tax-deferred accounts

MLPs pass the entire tax burden to investors. In an attempt to avoid this burden, you may consider putting your MLP in a tax-deferred account, but it doesn't do you much good. The IRS wants its cut, so it has set a $1,000 limit for taxable income from partnerships held in tax-deferred accounts. If you go over, the account gets hit with a big tax bill. That's right. The tax-deferred account has to pay a significant amount of taxes. Sorta defeats the purpose.

Don't put MLPs into tax-deferred accounts.

Calculating Your After-Tax Returns

The government is constantly fiddling with the tax code in an attempt to collect taxes without choking the life out of the economy. As a result, those tax incentives can go poof any time Congress decides to pull the plug or simply fails to renew the incentives before they expire. Some changes in the way returns are taxed can even tip the scales when you're trying to decide which investment is a better deal. Start taxing dividends as ordinary income, for example, and the number of companies paying dividends and the number of investors buying dividend stocks soon slump.

As the government fiddles with the tax code, be prepared to adjust your strategy accordingly. Crunch the numbers to determine your real (after-tax) return on a particular investment and see whether you can improve your real return by moving you money to a different investment type.

Here's a formula for calculating the after-tax return on an investment:

After-Tax Return = Percent Return × (1.00 − Percent Tax)

For example, if a particular investment earns you a 7.5 percent return and is taxed at 20 percent:

.075 × (1.00 – .20) = .06 or 6 percent

Suppose you own a dividend stock that's generating a total return of about 7 percent. Approximately 4 percent of that is from capital gains, and the other 3 percent is from dividends. Further, suppose you're paying 15-percent tax on both capital gains and dividends:

.07 × (1.00 – .15) = .0595 or 5.95 percent

Now, imagine you can purchase a bond that earns a 9-percent return but that's taxed as ordinary income at 35 percent:

.09 × (1.00 – .35) = .0585 or 5.85 percent

The two returns after taxes are pretty much a tossup. You may favor the bond because it's the same return with less risk, or you may favor the dividend stock because it has the potential of share price appreciation and dividend growth.

Now suppose the tax benefits of the JGTRRA (discussed earlier in the chapter) expire and you have the misfortune of having your income place you in the top income tax bracket. The after-tax return on your dividend stock suddenly looks a little less comparable. Your capital gains are now subject to a 20-percent tax, and your dividends are taxed as ordinary income at a rate of 38.6 percent:

.04 × (1.00 – .20) = .032 or 3.2 percent

.03 × (1.00 – .386) = .01842 or 1.842 percent

Adding those two figures together, your after-tax return is now slightly more than 5 percent, causing you to lean a little closer to investing in bonds.

Part IV
The Part of Tens

the
part of
tens

Are widows and orphans stocks still a stable choice?
Find out at www.dummies.com/extras/
investingindividends.

In this part . . .

- ✔ Check your facts and slay your misconceptions about dividends.

- ✔ Outsmart common mistakes, like getting too focused on yield or failing to keep an eye on the market.

Chapter 12

Ten Common Misconceptions about Dividends

Stock market investors and analysts often take sides on the issue of investing in dividend stocks. On one side are the cheerleaders who believe dividend stocks are the next best thing to free money. On the other are the naysayers who believe that dividend stocks are the next worst thing to a government takeover. Truth tends to lie somewhere in between. In this chapter, I bust the ten most common myths and misconceptions about investing in dividend stocks to provide you with a more balanced view.

Dividend Investing Is Only for Old, Retired Folks

Dividend investing is admittedly attractive for seniors, whose goals are typically capital preservation and income. Younger investors, however, can also benefit from a dividend investing model, even if it comprises only a portion of their portfolios.

Although seniors may want to stick with large, well-established corporations, younger investors may want to aim more toward the middle to lower end of the dividend spectrum. Younger investors wanting growth stocks should buy up-and-coming companies that are established enough to pay small dividends but demonstrate that they still have plenty of growth potential (in both capital appreciation and dividend payments).

Dividend investing isn't a get-rich-quick strategy. It's a great way to build wealth over the long term (which means you want to start when you're young) to secure a steady cash flow for your retirement years. Affluent older investors were young once, and many of them followed a relatively conservative dividend investment strategy even then to build their wealth.

I Can Get Better Returns with Growth Stocks

Although growth stocks may offer more in terms of share price appreciation, dividend stocks often make up the difference in dividend payments. Dividend stocks can see returns grow in three ways:

- ✔ Share prices can rise.
- ✔ Dividend payments can increase.
- ✔ Reinvested dividends can purchase more stock.

When comparing growth and dividend stocks, compare their potential in terms of *total* return on investment. For the dividend stock, this means share price appreciation *plus* dividends.

Sometimes, slow and steady really does win the race. Growth stocks may carry a higher potential for bigger returns, but they also carry a higher risk for bigger losses. If you do experience a loss, your other holdings need to perform that much better to make up the difference.

Dividend Stocks Are Safe Investments

Investing is risky no matter how you slice it; the risk of losing money is always present. However, some investments, including dividend stocks, tend to be safer than others. I say "tend to be" because even traditionally safer investment vehicles can take a hit. In 2009, for example, financials and real estate, which had paid reliable dividends for some time, went into a tailspin.

Don't put all your investment eggs in one basket. Even when investing in safer options, diversify to spread the risk among several sectors and among companies in the various industries you choose to invest in.

Companies Limit Their Growth by Paying Dividends

Growth investors often argue that companies paying dividends would be better off reinvesting that money to fuel their growth. Although this suggestion may be the case with some companies in certain situations, the reasoning is valid only if that money is well spent.

Companies that don't pay dividends give managers unrestricted use of the profits. Corporate executives often make acquisitions or start projects more to boost their personal worth (through bonuses and reputation) than to boost shareholder value. Risky acquisitions outside the company's main business often promise big results and just as often turn into money pits. Meanwhile, a commitment to paying dividends keeps management honest. Knowing the company must generate a certain amount of cash flow per quarter to pay the dividends shareholders expect tends to motivate management to manage effectively. In addition, paying dividends leaves management with less capital to squander on risky business ventures. As a result, management must evaluate prospective business ventures more carefully.

Some of the largest companies in the world pay dividends, and they didn't start out big. They began from scratch and grew; many continue to post significant growth despite paying dividends.

Paying Down Debt Always Comes Before Paying Dividends

Debt isn't necessarily a bad thing, although excessive debt certainly is. Whether a company should pay down debt before cutting dividend checks depends on the circumstances. If the company is buried in debt and struggling in a tough economy, paying down debt before paying dividends is not only a good idea but also an essential move to protect the company's survival. If, on the other hand, the company carries a reasonable debt load and its other fundamentals are solid, continuing or even raising dividend payments sends a positive message to the market.

Before purchasing a dividend stock, carefully inspect the company's quarterly reports and take a close look at the quick ratio, which I explain in Chapter 9. The *quick ratio* indicates whether the company's current assets are sufficient to cover its liabilities. The break-even point is a quick ratio of one, which usually means the company can afford to cover its liabilities, including its declared dividend payout. Anything less than one may mean that the company needs to borrow money to pay dividends, which is a bad sign.

Companies Must Maintain a Stable Dividend Payout

Companies are not obligated to pay dividends or to keep the payment stable after they start. However, dividend cuts tend to reflect poorly on a company and its share price, so companies tend to be conservative in establishing a dividend policy. Companies protect themselves by choosing a dividend payment method that allows them to manage shareholder expectations:

- ✓ **Residual:** With the *residual approach,* the company funds any new projects out of equity it generates internally and pays dividends only after meeting the capital requirements of these projects. In other words, investors receive a cut of the profits only if money is left over at the end of the quarter. Knowing this, investors are less likely to sell their shares if they don't receive a dividend payment for a particular quarter because they know next quarter may still bring a dividend.

- ✓ **Stability:** A *stability approach* sets the dividend at a fixed number, typically a fraction of quarterly or annual earnings, called a payout ratio. This gives investors a greater level of certainty that they'll receive a dividend and how much it's likely to be. Companies that implement a stable dividend payment approach tend to make conservative projections so that they don't disappoint shareholders.

- ✓ **Hybrid:** The *hybrid approach* is a combination of the residual and stability approaches. Companies that follow this approach tend to set a low, fixed dividend that they feel is easy to sustain and then distribute additional dividends when they can afford to do so.

My Dividend Increases Won't Even Keep Up with Inflation

Some companies' dividend increases do in fact fail to keep pace with inflation. Your goal as a dividend investor is to ensure that the dividend payments from companies you invest in at least keep up with inflation and hopefully exceed the inflation rate. If you're a growth investor looking for income, don't dump a stock just because dividend payments aren't keeping pace with inflation. Look at the stock's total return, including share price appreciation, and continue to monitor the company's fundamentals and the market at large. If the company is doing well, especially in a tough market, it may have the potential to raise dividend payments sometime in the future and perform well for you.

All Dividends Are Taxed at the Same Rate

As I discuss in Chapter 3, dividend investing fell out of favor in the 20th century because of unfavorable dividend taxation. A major reason for the resurgence of dividend investing was the lowering of the tax rate on dividends (20 percent or less during the writing of this book). The catch is that not all stocks qualify for the lower tax rate. To qualify, you have to hold the stock in your portfolio for at least 61 consecutive days during the 121-day period that begins 60 days before the ex-dividend date. Dividends that fail to qualify get taxed at the investor's regular tax rate. (One exception is master limited partnerships, which pass all their tax liabilities back to investors; check out Chapter 4 for more info.) For a full explanation about the tax issues regarding dividend stocks, visit Chapter 11.

The day on which you buy the stock doesn't count toward the 60-day holding requirement. Flip to Chapter 2 for more on important stock-purchasing dates.

You Should Always Invest in High-Yield Stocks

Don't judge a stock by yield alone. Yield is a valuable measure of how much bang you're getting for each of your investment bucks, but it alone doesn't determine a stock's true value; you also need to look at the share price. You can use a minimum yield to screen out stocks that don't meet your income requirements, but carefully evaluate a company's fundamentals before investing in it.

A high yield can mean many things — some positive, some negative. High yield may be a sign that the company's share price is sinking and that the company may be in trouble. If the high yield is out of whack with its sector, that may be a sign of an impending dividend cut. By the same token, don't immediately write off low-yield stocks.

REITs and Bank Stocks Are No Longer Good for Dividends

Two major factors that contributed to the fiscal crisis of 2008–2009 were a housing bubble that pushed the prices of real estate properties to astronomical heights and banks that approved mortgage loans for borrowers who couldn't afford the payments. Not surprisingly, real estate investment trusts (REITS) and bank stocks, traditionally big dividend payers, were some of the hardest hit in the stock market crash of 2008–2009. With little cash to pay their obligations, many REITs and banks were forced to cut or eliminate their dividends. However, a few strong companies continued to pay out dividends and even raised payments because they took less risk and managed their debt well. Don't write off all these companies in one fell swoop. Many have cleaned up their balance sheets and reinstated dividends.

Chapter 13

Ten Dividend Investing Mistakes to Avoid

*I*n the world of investing, you can never completely eliminate risk, but you can reduce it by making more good decisions and fewer bad ones. In this chapter, I highlight some of
the most common and serious dividend investing mistakes
you can make so that you can avoid them and improve
your odds.

Buying a Stock Solely on a Hot Tip

A hot tip is just that — a tip, an idea to follow up on. You still
need to do your research, which means you should pull up
the company's quarterly statements over the past year or
so, crunch the numbers, see whether any insiders are buying
shares, and perhaps even speak with one of the company's
representatives (or at least your broker) to check on the company's prospects moving forward.

Don't rely solely on the word of a friend, relative, colleague,
or even broker to choose which stocks to buy. Verify anything you hear with the kind of thorough personal research
I describe in Chapter 9.

Skipping Your Homework

Fear and greed often prevail on Wall Street, primarily because people tend to invest with their hearts rather than with their heads. They chase hot stocks when they should be avoiding them and then dump everything — good stocks and bad — when the sell-off starts. Those who win the day are the investors who do their homework and keep a cool head when everyone else is losing theirs.

The best way to keep a cool head is to know what you own, what you're buying, what you're selling, and why. If you know you own well-managed companies that have a solid track record for growing sales, profits, and dividend payments, you're less likely to get spooked when the market takes a dive. You can look for deals instead of looking for the exits.

Expecting to Buy and Sell Shares Just for the Dividend

Wouldn't it be great if you could buy a stock the day before the company is due to pay dividends, collect your dividend payment, and then sell the stock? On the surface, this strategy seems like a good way to beat the market, especially if the company has announced a big one-time dividend payout. Unfortunately, this clever trick doesn't work.

Sure, you may be able to collect the dividend payment, but when you try to sell the stock the next day, you'll be sorely disappointed. Share prices are reduced to reflect that dividend payout, and if you sell immediately after the dividend payment date, you pretty much break even.

Focusing Solely on Yield

When people start investing in dividend stocks, they automatically gravitate to the high-yield stocks. But depending on the industry, a high-yield stock can just as often be a sign of trouble as a sign of big profits. Don't let yield blind you to a company's growth prospects. Often, a company with a lower-than-average dividend that's experiencing solid growth and consistently increasing its dividend may be a better choice than a company with a larger yield that's currently in stagnation mode.

If you own a $10 stock paying a 2.5-percent yield, you receive 25 cents a year. If the share price and dividend payout both increase 10 percent each year, after ten years the stock would be worth $23.57, and the dividend payout would be 59 cents a year. Compared to current share price of $23.57, the yield remains 2.5 percent. But based on your original cost of $10 a share, the yield has more than doubled to 5.9 percent. Every time the dividend payout grows, not only does the yield on your initial investment grow, but your investment continues to beat inflation.

Don't buy a stock simply because it has a high yield. Find out whether the yield is high because of high dividend payments, low share price, or both. Examine the company's fundamentals as well as the broad market and economic environment. Perform additional research to ensure that the company is sound before you invest in it.

Focusing on Current Rather than Future Dividends

When you look up a stock's dividend, you're looking at its current dividend, which is like looking at yesterday's news. It's relevant because that's what you get paid this year. But as an investor, you're less interested in what the dividend's paying now and more interested in its potential to grow in the future. Unfortunately, nobody has a crystal ball to reveal how much a company will pay in dividends in the future, but you can make an educated prediction by examining the following:

- ✔ The company's recent and long-term trend in raising dividends
- ✔ Management's income projections
- ✔ Any significant developments that may alter the company's past trend of free cash flow

You may be better off buying shares in a company that pays a lower dividend if the company shows a lot of potential for raising its dividend moving forward, rather than a high dividend that remains static.

Failing to Monitor Stocks and the Market

Assuming you purchase stock in large, well-managed companies with a solid track record of paying dividends, you can sleep a little more soundly than most growth investors or Wall Street speculators. However, you shouldn't fall asleep at the wheel. Even big companies can fail. Just look at Bear Stearns, Lehman Brothers, and Chrysler.

Always keep tabs on your money, the stocks you've purchased, and the news. If you're open to hearing bad news, you can usually pick up on the warning signs before a massive sell-off. When you start hearing people in the know talking about impending bubbles, that's usually a good sign that you need to perk up your ears and make exit plans. Focus your plans not only on reducing risk but also on taking advantage of new opportunities.

Buying a Stock Just Because It's Cheap

Knowing the difference between a low share price and a good value is the difference between making and losing money. Just because a stock is cheap doesn't mean it's a bargain. Admittedly, buying a cheap stock is tempting. If shares are selling for 50 cents, you can scoop up 200 shares for a hundred bucks. In addition, you can more easily imagine 50-cent shares doubling in price than you can imagine shares selling for $100 a pop doubling in price. However, buying a stock just because it's cheap isn't investing. It's speculating or betting. Those 50-cent shares can just as easily lose half or all of their value, which is usually what happens.

To steer clear of this trap, carefully research a cheap stock's company fundamentals. Unlike large and higher-priced stocks, you usually find very little other information about these low-priced companies. In Chapter 9, I explain how you can determine a stock's intrinsic value and get a clearer idea of what you're buying and the company's prospects. Companies that have a history of paying dividends are rarely cheap, but when they are, that's a screaming buy. As long as you stick with the dividend investing model, you should be free of any temptation to buy a stock solely because it has a low share price.

Holding a Poor-Performing Stock for Too Long

Letting go is tough, especially if you own stock in a company that's performed well for you in the past or even one that experiences only short-lived highs. Waiting to sell until you get even is a loser's strategy. You don't keep fishing at a once-fertile fishing hole after the fish leave. You move on to a new spot. On Wall Street, emotional attachments can be brutal, and hope can be your true enemy. If a company has experienced a serious setback and is losing market share, don't let your emotions get in the way. Cut your losses, dump your shares, and find another place to invest your money.

How do you know when to get out? Here are a few guidelines:

- ✔ **If the company eliminates the dividend, get out immediately.** The company is in crisis mode.

- ✔ **If the company cuts the dividend, take a close look to get an idea of the company's growth prospects in light of this cut.** Selling this stock is a judgment call. If the cut comes because of broader economic conditions, you have to determine whether you believe this management team can steer the company through dangerous waters. If the cut is because of the company's internal problems, sell immediately.

- ✔ **If the company's share price drops more than 10 percent but the company maintains the dividend, do a little more investigation.** This situation is another judgment call. First, look at the rest of the market. Is the price down because of a sharp decline in the sector or broad market? Is this company part of the sector causing all the trouble?

  If during a market downturn your stock is part of a stronger, more defensive industry that continues to do business and should rally with the economy, hold on for the ride and consider buying more.

✔ **If the share price drops and the company boosts the dividend payout, buy more shares.**

Failing to Account for Taxes

Too many investors focus on the amount they stand to gain and don't stop to think about how big a bite taxes can take out of that figure. Financial success isn't necessarily based on how much money you earn. How much money you keep is what matters.

Regardless of where you put your money — stocks, bonds, real estate, CDs, money market funds, and so on — always consider the tax ramifications of your investment decisions. If you earn $200,000 and lose 35 percent in taxes, you walk away with $130,000. Pay only 15 percent in taxes, and you keep $170,000, or about 31 percent more. If you need to, talk to an accountant to develop a strategy that maximizes your after-tax returns. If the government decides to raise taxes on dividends to 30 percent, be prepared to adjust your strategy to take advantage of other investments with lower tax rates (if available, of course). Chapter 11 delves further into tax considerations.

Giving Too Much Credence to Media Reports and Analysis

Financial newspapers and magazines, websites, and investment TV and radio shows are all excellent sources of information, but they're not always right. That's because they rely on information from company insiders. If investors learned anything from the meltdown in the financial sector in 2008, it's that people lie and management isn't always forthcoming about what's going on in a company.

Don't assume any single source is 100-percent reliable. A company's financial documents are always the best source. Financial newspapers and their websites come second. But newspapers can make mistakes, too. Always verify the information by comparing it to other sources and your own instincts and insight.

Index

About the Author

Lawrence Carrel is an award-winning financial journalist and author of *ETFs for the Long Run: What They Are, How They Work, and Simple Strategies for Successful Long-Term Investing* (Wiley). He currently writes a blog of the same name at www. ETFsForTheLongRun.com.

After working as a newspaper reporter and editor, Carrel entered the online publishing business when financial news joined the Internet age. As a founding staff member of The Wall Street Journal.com, he was one of the original writers of its *Cyber Investing* column and among the first to write about small stocks for the Web. Later at SmartMoney.com, his daily market commentary tracked the dot-com bubble and the crash of 2000. A year later, he created *SmartMoney*'s daily online hot stocks column, *The One-Day Wonder*. Over five years, he reported on nearly 1,200 different companies in almost every industry. He later created two other columns for SmartMoney. com: *Under the Radar*, which looked for investments among small stocks, and *ETF Focus,* just as the exchange-traded fund (ETF) industry began its era of explosive growth. In 2007, he took over the weekly ETF and mutual fund columns at TheStreet.com. While there, Carrel predicted the 2008 stock market decline in August 2007 and told readers to start shorting the market with ETFs. He was also the first to report on the connection between the subprime mortgage crisis and the plunge in municipal bonds. His work has appeared in many top financial publications such as *Kiplinger Personal Finance Magazine, Investor's Business Daily, Barron's Online* and *Reuters Money.*

For three years, Carrel served as a daily contributor to *The Wall Street Journal This Morning* radio show and has been a guest commentator on MSNBC, CNN, and numerous other news networks. He has addressed the NASDAQ Stock Market as an ETF expert, and served as a founding featured journalist on The Investor Network, a social network for investors. In a break from financial journalism, Carrel worked as a contributing editor on the college humor compilation, *Lunacy: The Best of the Cornell Lunatic* (Lunatic Press). A native of Buffalo, New York, and a graduate of Cornell University, he lives in New York City with his two sons.

Dedication

To Judy Hayes, who believed in me when no one else did.

Author's Acknowledgments

Thanks to acquisitions editor Stacy Kennedy, who chose me to author this book, and exhibited incredible patience, faith, and understanding during the process. I'm extremely grateful to Joe Kraynak, a gifted editor and collaborator, who was instrumental in helping me complete this book; my wonderful agent, Marilyn Allen at Allen O'Shea Literary Agency, for getting me on this project; and Russell Wild, for recommending me to Marilyn.

Thanks to Alissa Schwipps, my gifted project editor for the first edition, and copy editor Megan Knoll for ferreting out my language foe paws (or is it faux pas?). I also tip my hat to the production crew for doing such an outstanding job of transforming a loose collection of matchbook covers, napkins, scraps of paper, and illustrations into such an attractive bound book. Also, thanks to original technical editor Noel Jameson.

I want to thank the following people for giving their time to help me acquire the information necessary to write this book: Stuart Bell of WisdomTree Investments, Gary Bradshaw of Hodges Capital Management, John Buckingham of Al Frank Asset Management, Jennifer Connelly of JCPR, Anthony Corrao of Oppenheimer & Co., Lauren DeSanto of Morningstar, Jaime Doyle of SunStar, Mark Farber of Weiser LLP., Tom Forsha of Aston/RiverRoad Dividend All Cap Value Fund, Dan Genter of RNC Genter Capital Management, Carol Grauman of JCPR, David Guarino of Standard & Poor's, Kathryn Hyatt of The Vanguard Group, Frank Ingarra of the Hennessey Funds, Rebecca Katz of The Vanguard Group, Naomi Kim of Dow Jones Indexes, Tony Kono of SunStar, Annette Larson of Morningstar, John R. Lieberman of Perelson Weiner LLP., Ivy McLemore of Invesco Aim, Melissa Murphy of SunStar, Vita Nelson of The MoneyPaper, Lisa Osofsky of Weiser LLP., Rebecca Patterson of Dow Jones Indexes, Josh Peters of Morningstar, Steven M. Rogé of R. W. Rogé & Co., Bill Rogers of Mergent, Tom Roseen of ThomsonReuters, Henry Sanders of Aston/RiverRoad Dividend All Cap Value Fund, Jeremy Schwartz of WisdomTree Investments, Kevin Shacknofsky of

Alpine Funds, Howard Silverblatt of Standard & Poor's, Jordan Smyth Jr. of Edgemoor Investment Advisors, Nadine Youssef of Morningstar, and William Zimmerman of Morgan, Lewis & Bockius.

I also want to thank my friends and family for their love and support: Kirsten Mogg, Jackson Carrel, Janice Carrel, Jerome Carrel, Judy Carrel, Marc Carrel, Theo Carrel, Darrin Greene, Nick Wade, Steven Fox for his legal help, and Greg Candela for the beer. I also owe an enormous amount of gratitude to Sterling Barrett and Joe Barello, who saved this project by procuring for me on short notice a top-notch computer when both my desktop and laptop died a week before this book was due.

Publisher's Acknowledgments

Acquisitions Editor: Stacy Kennedy

Compiler: Traci Cumbay

Project Editor: Tim Gallan

Project Editor (previous edition): Alissa Schwipps

Copy Editor (previous edition): Megan Knoll

Art Coordinator: Alicia B. South

Production Editor: Kumar Chellappan

Cover Image: © Singkham/Shutterstock

Math & Science

Algebra I For Dummies, 2nd Edition
978-0-470-55964-2

Anatomy and Physiology For Dummies, 2nd Edition
978-0-470-92326-9

Astronomy For Dummies, 3rd Edition
978-1-118-37697-3

Biology For Dummies, 2nd Edition
978-0-470-59875-7

Chemistry For Dummies, 2nd Edition
978-1-118-00730-3

1001 Algebra II Practice Problems For Dummies
978-1-118-44662-1

Microsoft Office

Excel 2013 For Dummies
978-1-118-51012-4

Office 2013 All-in-One For Dummies
978-1-118-51636-2

PowerPoint 2013 For Dummies
978-1-118-50253-2

Word 2013 For Dummies
978-1-118-49123-2

Music

Blues Harmonica For Dummies
978-1-118-25269-7

Guitar For Dummies, 3rd Edition
978-1-118-11554-1

iPod & iTunes For Dummies, 10th Edition
978-1-118-50864-0

Programming

Beginning Programming with C For Dummies
978-1-118-73763-7

Excel VBA Programming For Dummies, 3rd Edition
978-1-118-49037-2

Java For Dummies, 6th Edition
978-1-118-40780-6

Religion & Inspiration

The Bible For Dummies
978-0-7645-5296-0

Buddhism For Dummies, 2nd Edition
978-1-118-02379-2

Catholicism For Dummies, 2nd Edition
978-1-118-07778-8

Self-Help & Relationships

Beating Sugar Addiction For Dummies
978-1-118-54645-1

Meditation For Dummies, 3rd Edition
978-1-118-29144-3

Seniors

Laptops For Seniors For Dummies, 3rd Edition
978-1-118-71105-7

Computers For Seniors For Dummies, 3rd Edition
978-1-118-11553-4

iPad For Seniors For Dummies, 6th Edition
978-1-118-72826-0

Social Security For Dummies
978-1-118-20573-0

Smartphones & Tablets

Android Phones For Dummies, 2nd Edition
978-1-118-72030-1

Nexus Tablets For Dummies
978-1-118-77243-0

Samsung Galaxy S 4 For Dummies
978-1-118-64222-1

Samsung Galaxy Tabs For Dummies
978-1-118-77294-2

Test Prep

ACT For Dummies, 5th Edition
978-1-118-01259-8

ASVAB For Dummies, 3rd Edition
978-0-470-63760-9

GRE For Dummies, 7th Edition
978-0-470-88921-3

Officer Candidate Tests For Dummies
978-0-470-59876-4

Physician's Assistant Exam For Dummies
978-1-118-11556-5

Series 7 Exam For Dummies
978-0-470-09932-2

Windows 8

Windows 8.1 All-in-One For Dummies
978-1-118-82087-2

Windows 8.1 For Dummies
978-1-118-82121-3

Windows 8.1 For Dummies, Book + DVD Bundle
978-1-118-82107-7

Available in print and e-book formats.

Available wherever books are sold.

For more information or to order direct visit www.dummies.com

Take Dummies with you everywhere you go!

Whether you are excited about e-books, want more from the web, must have your mobile apps, or are swept up in social media, Dummies makes everything easier.

For Dummies is the global leader in the reference category and one of the most trusted and highly regarded brands in the world. No longer just focused on books, customers now have access to the For Dummies content they need in the format they want. Let us help you develop a solution that will fit your brand and help you connect with your customers.

Advertising & Sponsorships

Connect with an engaged audience on a powerful multimedia site, and position your message alongside expert how-to content.

Targeted ads • Video • Email marketing • Microsites • Sweepstakes sponsorship

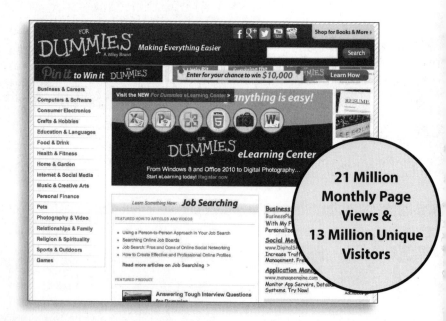